Manchmal in der unaufhörlich greifenden Noth dieser Tage überragt, mich etwas mit der ~~[illegible]~~ vorausleuchtende Schein einer neuen geistigen Kraft: als ob doch Alles u. einfacher geworden sei und ein unsägliches Schicksal in Annäherungsmomenten sich faßlicher mache. Denn ist es schließlich nicht dies, (wenn man es aussprechen soll): daß Helle und Dunkelheit in meinem Innern nicht durch eines Menschen überwiegenden Einfluß bestimmt werden dürfen, sondern allein durch ein Namenloses. Dies ist, sozusagen, das Mindestmaß meiner Frömmigkeit: es aufgebend, müßte ich hinter den ersten Kreuzweg meines Lebens zurück –, hinter seine früheste stillste ~~[illegible]~~ ~~[illegible]~~ Entscheidung. Hinter mich selbst.

freieste

(Briefentwurf)

Schloss B..., ohne Datum:

immer.

Mein Geliebter, wem, wenn nicht Dir, soll ich diesen schweren Abschluss meines Herzens anvertrauen? Wenn er Dich in Noth versetzt, bedenke, wie groß die Noth sein muss, aus der heraus ich das Folgende aufschreibe.

Ich habe Unrecht gethan; Verrath. Ich habe die Umstände, die mir nach sechs Jahren der Zerstörung und Hinderung mit B... geboten waren, nicht ausgenutzt für die unaufschiebbare innere Aufgabe; sie ist mir vom Schicksal unter den Händen entwunden worden. Das muss ich mir nun eingestehen.

Du weißt, Liebe, wie mir jene Umstände, vom Zufälligsten bis ins (Letzte) Wesentlichste, zusagten, wie entschlossen ich sie antrat. Du wolltest das Deine thun, sie mir zu schützen:

The Testament

The Testament (& Other Texts)

Rainer Maria Rilke

Edited by Rainer J. Hanshe

Translation & Introduction by Mark Kanak

Contra Mundum Press New York · London · Melbourne

The Testament (& Other Texts)

— Rainer Maria Rilke, *Das Testament,* first published by Insel Verlag Frankfurt am Main, 1974.

First Contra Mundum Press edition 2025.

Library of Congress Cataloguing-in-Publication Data

Rilke, Rainer Maria, 1875–1926.
The Testament (& Other Texts) / Rainer Maria Rilke
—1st Contra Mundum Press Edition

202 pp., 5×8 in.

ISBN 9781940625805

I. Rilke, Rainer Maria.
II. Title.
III. Kanak, Mark.
IV. Translator.
V. Hanshe, Rainer J.
VI. Editor.

2025944215

TABLE OF CONTENTS

TRANSLATOR'S INTRODUCTION

Rilke's Testament of Solitude

If some of the shorter pieces included in this volume have been published in English translation, the central and longest one has not, and so, *The Testament (& Other Texts)* marks the first time they are gathered together in a single book, and this on the 150th anniversary of the poet's birth and one year in advance of the 100th anniversary of his death. The material comes from a unique period in Rainer Maria Rilke's life where, having endured the tumultuous & devastating war years, he was searching for the solitude required to complete his magnum opus, *The Duino Elegies*, which he had begun in January 1912 at Duino Castle, near Trieste. The poet's restless vagabondage and penurious situation certainly contributed to his bouts of depression and occasional ill health, and though he was constantly searching for the moment and location to dedicate himself to his task, no real opportunities had arisen. Prior to the ultimate completion of the well-known lyric revelations of the *Duino Elegies* and the luminous density of the *Sonnets to Orpheus* in February 1922, Rilke created quieter, often overlooked works — elliptical, speculative, half-lit by metaphysical inquiry and half-rooted in the perduring matter of earthly life. If the short, philosophical piece "Primal Sound" (October 1919) and the long, anonymous "Letter from a Young Worker" (February 1922) are the key texts in this phase, then the core of the arc comprising a transition in Rilke's late voice is *The Testament* (April/May 1921) and the poem cycle *"From the Literary Estate of Count C.W."* (November 1920 / April 1921). Taken together, these works comprise a trajectory leading to his greatest achievements as a poet.

At the end of 1918, the war years had disrupted not only Rilke's outer life, but his inner one as well: conscription, displacement, and spiritual injury had left the poet isolated and creatively blocked. By early 1919, he was recovering in Switzerland, adrift between sanatoriums and small villages, unmoored but receptive to any sign that might provide the impetus he needed to continue his work in earnest. If only for a fleeting moment, his heart was also keyed more to the world. Although the short piece that opens this collection, "(Draft of a Political Speech)," may seem incidental, it conveys a social and psychological consciousness perhaps unique for Rilke, one that stretches beyond the confines of the artist's monastic spaces and evokes in part the work of Freud,

Jung, and Reich. The hour of the age has struck midnight, a bell stroke that to the poet offers the promise of a new future, but one with an exigent task. The quintessential element of five years of global horror, injustice, and death ("the most deathly kind of death," he says) is an immeasurable pain, but one that has been repressed, "disconnected from any inner continuity of life." Endangered by this lack of discharge and psychic unity, the neutered senses unable to grasp the invisible, Rilke expresses a deep-felt need for civilization to break through its character armor and undergo a cathartic exorcism. Without it, there can be no peace, and no free future.

In the midst of seeking such catharsis himself, in this moment of retreat and exhaustion following his psychological collapse, the poet received a letter from Hans Prinzhorn — the psychiatrist and art historian known for collecting the works of his patients — asking him whether he believed in a kind of primal sound. The resulting response was in fact entitled just that, "Primal Sound" (Ur-Geräusch), and comprised a curious, luminous reply. The text imagines a phonograph needle running along a groove, producing vibration — and from that vibration, a sound so ancient & fundamental it might predate language itself. Rilke proposes this as a metaphor for resonance beneath perception, for something the world utters before we interpret it. But the gesture is more than acoustic; it is metaphysical. In listening for the primal sound, Rilke listens for the lost thread of connection — to being, to memory, to the pre-verbal self. In his 1844-essay (the year of Nietzsche's birth), "The Poet," Emerson speaks to this Orphic praxis when declaring that "poetry was all written before time was, and wherever we are so finely organized that we can penetrate into that region where the air is music, we hear those primal warblings and attempt to write them down…" When stating that "the men of more delicate ear write down these cadences more faithfully, and these transcripts, though imperfect, become the songs of the nations," Emerson could have been speaking of Rilke *avant la lettre*. As someone with more of an attuned ear, Rilke was able to perceive such music, and "Primal Sound" anticipates the dense sonic architecture of the *Sonnets to Orpheus*, but at this point, it is only a tentative signal: a vibration signaling through fog. The essay was not poetry; it was philosophy in miniature, speculation as survival, an attempt to sense the primal warblings.

What mattered was not the sound itself, but the idea that listening — *real listening*, what Heidegger called hearkening to being — can carry us toward what we've forgotten. "Primal Sound" is not then just the guiding tonality of this collection, but the prelude to Rilke's full re-entry into the world: not through image or symbol, but through pulse.

*

At the end of a decade of death, turmoil, and destruction, Rilke had already feared that he would never be able to complete the *Duino Elegies*. The outbreak of World War I had brought work to a standstill for more than a year when the poet was conscripted into military service; writing resumed only in the fall of 1915, resulting in the Fourth Elegy, written in one sitting in Munich in November. Yet, even after Rilke was discharged in the summer of 1916, the voices remained inert. He could no longer work every day as a craftsman, as Rodin had counseled him to do. The poet could not, it seems, access the images imprisoned within him; the new turning point had yet to arrive. It wasn't until the fall of 1918 that he would finally entrust clean copies of the pieces he had worked out or begun up to that point to his publisher Anton Kippenberg and his dear friend Lou Andreas-Salomé. Not much later, Rilke moved from Munich to Switzerland (the summer of 1919), a shift in locale and personal space that gave the poet hope that he would be able to create the living and working conditions necessary for his main task. This goal finally seemed to have been achieved when, at the beginning of his second post-war winter in Switzerland, a benefactress offered him a remote castle in the Canton of Zurich (Berg am Irchel) as a temporary residence. He would end up living there for half a year from November 12, 1920 to May 10, 1921. From the very first day, he realized that he had found the refuge he had long been seeking. The concentration he quickly achieved soon allowed him to complete some preliminary works, such as the French-language "Préface Mitsou / Quarante images par Balthusz" (referenced in *The Testament*) and the cycle of poems included in this volume, "From the Literary Estate of Count C.W." (*Aus dem Nachlaß des Grafen C.W.*).

During this time, Rilke was invited to present his work at the Zürich Readers' Circle at Hottingen, an occasion that gives us his "Preface to a Reading from my Own Works."

Prior, Rilke explains that he found poetry too narrow and limited, and had ceased giving public readings for a decade. Out of a newfound desire to communicate, in the midst of an exigent *kairos* that he believed required counsel, the poet sought to offer some aid. And so he expresses a phenomenological poetics born of his attunement with the world, his experience of death, both on a mass scale and intimately (the death of close friends: Countess Louise Schwerin (1906), Paula Modersohn-Becker (1907)), if not his sensitivity to the animal kingdom. Rilke expresses his conviction that one of his rightful tasks is "to reveal the breadth, the vastness, indeed the completeness of the world in distilled expressions." A poem is to be a testimony of affect *and* phenomenon which, "in a lyrical manner," portray things (animal, plant, process, etc.) not only in their own "peculiar emotional-space." In this, Rilke is enacting his notion of *Einsehen* (seeing-into), which is not a form of passive reception, but more a kind of shamanic absorption and self- or thingly-doubling through which dwelling is established. As Michael Worton noted, it is by projecting oneself "into the Other," "by echoing actively and passively the 'irreducible Other's' voice, by being simultaneously present and absent, 'the same' and 'different' as Heidegger would say, that we establish any sense of our *Dasein*, of our indwelling."[1] The months in Switzerland however proved unsettling, a discombobulating excursus. His new-found focus broken, Rilke writes to his publisher of his need for order and security, wondering, "when shall I find these things, so necessary to my great task, and where?"

Precisely what disrupted his creative focus (in early December 1920 and around New Year 1920/1921) can only be noted in general terms here. At the time, Rilke had been involved with the poet and painter Baladine Klossowska (mother of Balthus and Pierre Klossowski), who he called "Merline." For Rilke, at first, the winter in Berg had seemed full of promise, but the apparent solitude the little manor might have initially offered proved to be illusory. As always, in prelude to serious work, the poet threw himself into an outpouring of correspondence with friends, patrons, and supporters. Although he was not idle creatively,

1. Michael Worton, "Windows onto Painting: Char's Writings on Art," *Art Criticism by French Poets Since World War II* (Dalhousie French Studies, Vol. 21, Fall–Winter 1991) 33.

the C.W. poems and the preface to Balthus's drawings were trifles in comparison to his real life's work.

Rather than personal solace and creative surges, what in fact did come was a steady flow of visitors and other distractions. In *The Testament*, Rilke references this when he speaks of "his nearly public apartment, plagued by visits from strangers & casual acquaintances alike." The most disruptive event however was the news that Merline was suffering from lumbago. Though in the name of his work he resisted the urge to visit her, he eventually relented, and their intention to remain apart for six months was interrupted when she spent some time recuperating at Berg. If seen by some critics as a creative obstacle, Merline might have indirectly served as a generative force when she gave Rilke a Christmas gift of Ovid's *Metamorphosis* in 1920 (a French translation which included the episodes of the Orpheus cycle) and a postcard of Orpheus. Did this (in some way, and if only indirectly) help crystallize the ideas that enabled Rilke to see his Orpheus cycle in a form appropriate to his poetic voice? Whether obstacle or muse, Merline's continuing influence is to be reckoned with. Her being the unnamed addressee of the draft letters included in *The Testament*, in particular the final draft with the heading "*Castle B, . . . , undated: forever*," seem to attest to Rilke's recognition of her impact. And the overall structure of this final section of *The Testament* corresponds to the preliminary recounting by the unnamed third party, to whom we owe the preservation and comprehensibility of the fragmentary texts. By placing the entire series of "testamentary" texts in the hands of his friend at their conclusion, with a turn of phrase reminiscent of Hölderlin's "To whom else but you," Rilke all but implies this. If he could not yet complete his *Elegies*, was Merline an obstacle, or was she but one element that enabled him to begin this preparatory work, the experimental writing of the *Testament*, work that would lead to an even greater creative outflowing? One might well view the *Testament*, which remained unpublished for 50 years in Germany, as the esoteric companion to both his letters to Merline and as the esoteric prelude to the *Duino Elegies*.

*

When suffering from acute distress over the creative impasse with his cycle of poems, Rilke compelled himself in the spring of 1921 to explore his own "mortality," which threatened to thwart his creativity time and again and which culminated in *The Testament*. These notes were not only born of a need to hold himself to account for his failures and shortcomings, but also of a desire to seal his deepest "will" as his "last" for future generations, in an extreme understanding of the conflict between fate and duty. Given the chaotic and unpredictable circumstances of the post-war years, there was ample reason for an author in Rilke's dire situation and mental state to seriously expect the ultimate failure of his much-endangered life's work. In such a tense case, at least the testimony of his conscience could one day be found amid the void left by his poetic legacy.

For somewhere there is an ancient enmity
between life and great work.
That I recognize it and say: help me.

These lines from the Ninth Elegy are a reminder of human and artistic greatness, and interpret the fate of one who passes on from an insight into the irrevocable conflict between the demands of the artistic task and those of life and love. From early on, Rilke saw himself as a poet and as a human being caught up in this very struggle. "Everyone," he wrote in a letter to Countess Mirbach-Geldern on March 10, 1921, "ultimately experiences only one conflict in life, which always appears in different guises and emerges in different places — my conflict is to reconcile life with work in the purest sense; when it comes to the infinite, incommensurable work of the artist, the two directions stand in opposition to each other." Similarly, around the same time (February 17, 1921), to Princess Marie von Thurn und Taxis: "Ultimately, it is always this one, in my experience irreconcilable conflict between life and work that I suffer in new, unheard-of variations and can hardly endure."

Rilke preceded the apparently unstructured collection of *The Testament* with an introduction written in the tone of a reporter who had discovered the disparate texts and felt obliged to give them a kind of guiding frame. Thus, the preface by the fictitious curator outlines the circumstances and coincidences that determined the life of the "writer" of these notes since the outbreak of the First World War. The distance between this fictitious witness and the person actually affected and his fate is evident in the discreet and knowledgeable character of the biographical third-person account, wherein facts, events, and connections are carefully, even laboriously described while the names of countries, places, and persons are omitted and merely hinted at or suggested to the reader. Only at the end of his introduction, when the past tense shifts to the present and future, do the narrative and interpretation of the supposed guarantor merge into the personal view of the confessor and the person he consults, namely, the "writer."

After its completion, the existence of the manuscript was hardly general knowledge. During his lifetime, Rilke entrusted a clean copy to Kippenberg, who later passed it on to the poet's heirs after Rilke's death. In the correspondence with Merline (May 19 & 26, 1921), there are brief mentions of the "notes" that he had scribbled down in Berg and that he would "one day" share with her. Rilke initially kept the manuscript to himself, and subsequently entrusted it to Nanny Wunderly-Volkart, also a patron and the executor of his estate, who eventually passed it on to the Rilke Archive at the Swiss National Library in Bern.

At the time, there was agreement among the small circle of people who knew about this document that its existence should be kept confidential for the time being.

The Testament occupies a special place in the poet's oeuvre and literary legacy. The title and the autobiographical introduction expressly confirm that we are not dealing with a personal, practical document, but with a self-testimony intended for posterity. Whether this should be classified as part of his artistic work in the strictest sense or rather included in his diaries and personal notes is open to debate; when the structure of Rilke's "Complete Works" was being conceived, it was ultimately decided to include this document in the diaries section. However, the nature of the composition clearly lends it the character of a work of art in two respects: the framework with its means of objectifying distancing, its elevation to the anonymous and exemplary, and the actual "notes" — in stark contrast — through the use of fragmentation as a principle of form and composition. The language also has the character of a creative endeavor, which becomes all the more apparent when one tries to understand and appreciate it against the background of the correspondence with "Merline."

Now, 50 years after its first publication in Germany, and over 100 years after its date of composition, the translation of this work into English offers Anglophone readers insight into this interregnum in Rilke's creative life.

*

During his stay at the castle, Rilke also worked on a collection of poems, which were written in two sections of similar length, in very brief creative bursts, with the first section being completed over three days in November 1920 and the second in March 1921. Partly because of Rilke's subsequently distancing himself from this work, and partly because the collection of poems offers little that is new in terms of subject matter, *"Aus dem Nachlaß des Grafen C.W."* ("From the Literary Estate of Count C.W.") is a desideratum of Rilke scholarship, although the cycle of poems represents an interesting precursor to the completion of the *Duino Elegies*. During Rilke's lifetime, the collection remained unpublished, except for one poem – the seventh in the first series, "In Karnak," which the poet published anonymously in the Insel Almanach – and was not published in Germany in its entirety until 1950, twenty-four years after Rilke's death.

It is clear that, with *The Testament* and the "Count C.W." poems, Rilke was actively working through his creative and spiritual crisis. Shortly after settling in, seeking inspiration in the castle library, he had discovered little of interest apart from works by Goethe and therefore invented the Count, making him the medium for his own memories, experiences, adventures, & melancholies. For Rilke, the poems were probably above all a kind of playful metafictional language exercise, as can be seen from a remark in a letter to Wunderly-Volkart dated November 30, 1920: "... the poems you see — on the first page you will read 'From the Literary Estate of Count C.W.' Curious things for which, pleasantly enough, I bear no responsibility whatsoever." The collection of poems could be characterized as a lyrical counterpart to Rilke's novel *The Notebooks of Malte Laurids Brigge* and contains the fragmentary, autobiographical memories of the mysterious "former resident of Berg," in lyrical form, occasionally commented on by the editor, which provides these "discovered" poems with an aura of "fictional authenticity."

The collection was clearly a playful writing experiment, the fictional protagonist a dilettante, as Rilke ironically admits in a letter to Wunderly-Volkart (November 30, 1920). The poet explains that he had been searching for documents belonging to the former owner in the 17th-century castle. After his efforts proved fruitless, he decided to slip into the role of a fictional former castle owner. He noted that he had written the accompanying cycle of poems, which he dismissively referred to as "*Spielerei*" (playfulness), in just three days. The collection of poems is significant in that it deals with motifs & subjects that later become themes in the *Duino Elegies*:

> Only now do I understand how it could have happened, day after day: not yet capable of producing anything myself and forced to do so, I had to make myself, as it were, "prominent" in a certain way, taking upon myself what could already be shaped at this highly inaccessible stage of concentration: that was Count C.W. A dilettante, strictly speaking. He writes many things that I would never have approved of, that is his business, and he is often clumsy, like all dilettantes — but in some things, in a few "great lines," he has my approval,

> indeed, to be honest, he has aroused my envy – in that he sometimes ends up being very close to me.

Like the cycle of poems, this letter is characterized by a playful oscillation between distance and empathy. Although the count is an amateur poet, he occasionally adumbrates Rilke's artistic style. He transports the Count's fictional poems and fragments of memory to the 19th century, as the poem "Schöne Aglaja, Freundin meiner Gefühle" ("Beautiful Aglaja, Friend of My Feelings") makes clear with the indication "Palermo 1862." This single date in the cycle serves to enhance the conceit.

For Rilke, fiction was a game with his own identity, as the count's initials could refer to two of Rilke's own names: "Carl" & "Wilhelm." This play with identity is a recurring concept in Rilke's work and allows him to identify or fuse with other figures, such as a Russian monk and icon painter in the *Book of Hours*, an officer in the Austrian imperial army of the 17th century in *The Way of Love and Death of Cornet Christoph Rilke*, a Danish nobleman in Paris in the *Notebooks of Malte Laurids Brigge*, and a young worker in "Letter from a Young Worker." Thematically, these poems, which are quite different in and of themselves, have in common that they are set in a particular season — the first half represents "autumn thoughts," the second "spring inventions." Formally, the predominantly four-line quatrains refer, among other things, to the early poetry collections *Larenopfer* (1895), *Traumgekrönt* (1896), and *Advent* (1897), as well as to Rilke's French poems *Vergers, Les Quatrains*, and *Valaisans* (1926).

Rilke's modeling of the role of the poet was influenced by Novalis and Hölderlin, among others; his aim is to bring the slumbering spirit of Orpheus back to life, to be the poet who hears the primal warblings. Similarly, in a letter to Princess von Thurn und Taxis (December 15, 1920), Rilke described the genesis of the poem cycle as a "dictation," with him appearing here as a medium who is "guided" by a higher power; Rilke particularly emphasizes the aforementioned poem "In Karnak," which refers biographically to his trip to Egypt in 1911:

> It was very strange — the pen was literally "guided" by me, poem after poem, except for a few places where one would recognize me; it was neither my style nor my opinion that was expressed there in its finished form

> (I wrote it *sans brouillon* in the notebook itself). There is a very beautiful (Egyptian) poem among them that I would very much like to have written. This happened in the space of three evenings, and on the second evening, I wrote fluently, without a moment's hesitation, on the title page: "From the Literary Estate of Count C.W." (as in the dictation) without thinking of a name to go with these initials, but absolutely certain that this was it. What was all this?"

The count's individual dreams and fragments of memory appear disparate and incomprehensible. Free associations, absurd dream fragments, and the oscillation between dream and reality form a heterogeneous unity. The poems remain fascinating if, for no other reason, than that they illuminate the circumstances of their creation and Rilke's inner condition while in Berg.

*

In a letter Rilke wrote to Merline on May 26, 1921, about two weeks after leaving Schloss Berg, the poet speaks of a destiny that supersedes the self:

> There is, I know it well, a greatness of pure destiny that goes so far beyond us that we are not even allowed to take blame upon ourselves within it. Nothing small, nothing demeaning has happened to us, my Beloved, but rather something great. If you need any consolation, let it be this: everything else that it may be for me, you must leave to me! I can neither share it nor talk about it — one day, the notes I wrote down at Berg the week before last will tell you something; the last part is not there, either; God forbid that it should ever be put into words, I couldn't bear it.

During his stay at Berg, Rilke had acutely begun to fear that his work would never be completed, and he wrote *The Testament* to that effect, blaming his failure in part on the terrible distractions of love. This fear is so intense, he speaks in *The Testament* of empty white pages as being "so sinister..." It would only be in early 1922, at Muzot, that the floodgates finally broke and Rilke would write, in a feverish creative outpouring, the *Sonnets to Orpheus* and the conclusion to his *Duino Elegies*. Rilke's jubilant cry of "I am saved!" — penned in a letter to

Merline, who had left for Berlin to grant him the solitude so desperately missing in Berg – marked the moment of triumph after years of frustration. That brief eruption of creative clarity not only redeemed his earlier artistic failures, but also silenced the long torment of his self-doubt. And in a February 11, 1922 letter to Lou Andreas-Salomé – the very evening he completed the *Duino Elegies* –, with an urgency that suggests both creative submission and a fear of mortality, Rilke wrote of "... a boundless storm, a hurricane of the spirit – and whatever inside me is like thread & webbing, framework, it all cracked and bent ...."

*

All in all, the exploratory phase of 1919–1922 marked a decisive shift, the longed-for turning point, and is reflected in Rilke's late style: after years of searching and sporadic writing, the poet had finally reached *the* moment of clarity and urgency. His correspondence from this time often mirrors the spiritual intensity and transformative tone found in his 1922 poems, which was his creative zenith. "Letter from a Young Worker" dates to the same creative surge of that crucial February at Muzot, showcasing his mature voice — theological, lyrical, earthy — and stands beside the *Elegies* and *Sonnets* as a key artifact of that extraordinary period. It extends the themes of embodiment, labor, erotics, and the sacral everyday into the realm of the modern world (factories, machines, mistrust of organized religion), all of which would figure in George Bataille's later work on erotism. Crucially, Rilke's fictitious letter ends not in abstraction, but in a desire to offer one's work to God — echoing *Orpheus*, but from below rather than above, and is a kind of chthonic pagan prayer to the earth where sexuality isn't tainted with sin or guilt, but is an energizing center of life. At the height of psychoanalytic fervor, Rilke expresses here, in his own terms, something akin to Freud's conception of libido.

Rilke considered "Letter from a Young Worker" to be important enough to have it published the very same month of its composition in the *Neue Schweizer Rundschau* journal. To reinforce the significance he gave it, we made it the coda to our collection, for in it, all the vibrations, reflections, and inward journeys of the earlier texts are filtered through lived experience, into a speech that cracks through the margins: humble, lucid, and charged with pagan elegance. The text was something of a companion piece — not in style or form, but in existential weight, and expressed many concerns that the *Elegies* orbit: divinity, immanence, transformation, the sacred within suffering and ordinary life. Yet where the *Elegies* speak from the heights (spirit), the "Letter" speaks from lower, more ordinary, or bodily realms.

Reading this group of six texts as a sextet where primal vibration and social prayer are reflected, reveals a hitherto unseen compositional unity and creative thrust to a supposed fallow period. At the time, Rilke himself didn't even seem aware of this unconscious dynamism and how his *prose thinking* prior to the completion of the *Elegies* and *Sonnets* was expressed in a quieter, stranger way. Nonetheless, it contains much of the same ecstatic threshold and, taken together, can be (partially) viewed as a grounded counterpart to the cosmic tone of Rilke's more prominent works. The reflection on the nature of the original conflict recorded in his "testament" penetrates deeper and leads further than the poet had succeeded in doing at earlier stages, even in the above-mentioned

February and March 1921 letters. The reduction of the ever-present "old enmity" between life and work against the background of the conflict in the midst of one's own capacity for love 'simplified,' one might say, the urgency of Rilke's impending fate and defined it acutely: "la coïncidence de deux félicités extrêmes, voilà son nom —": "the coincidence of two extreme felicities, that is its name —"

Berlin, August 2025
Mark Kanak

The Testament
(& Other Texts)

(Draft of a Political Speech)

[Midsummer or Autumn 1919]

The political clock resembles those watchman's clocks which, unless tampered with by fools or frauds, are set to register signs of vigilance; they mark a stationary, relative, comparative time, not actually the universal time. And now everyone is asking: what time is it?

If midnight has passed — a true midnight for the world — then, even in the darkness, a singular, firm stroke follows: One! with it, the first promise of a new day is given into our hands, so that we might begin to prepare its fulfillment.

But when we look at the faces of those who raise their eyes toward the other clock — the political one — it is impossible to know what is happening. The monstrous events, achievements, and obligations of the war have moved, one by one, onto a provisional plane — they stand larger than life, and yet they do not possess the magnitude of nature. The perspective recalibrates, & a modest tree once again appears taller than heroism.

The provisional nature, the indented nature of those horrific five years, will most urgently become clear to you if I show you how, from the very beginning, the only real thing in them was not permitted to be accomplished: pain.

I dare not say this in a country that was directly ensnared in that monstrous disaster – for who could bear the responsibility of reminding those bound by pain that they had not yet fully discharged their measure of tears?

But here, in Switzerland – which, as a compassionate and humane presence, was allowed to offer sympathy and support in all directions, while other nations were condemned to one hatred or another, or to ever more hatred – here, it is possible to say, with infinite compassion, that in those accursed lands, sums of money for suffering of unprecedented magnitude, which were due, have been embezzled.

The idea of sacrifice, the harsh pride, the continual reinterpretation of disaster, which was disaster still, of so much injustice, which remained injustice, of so much death, which was nothing but death, and the most deathly kind of death, disconnected from any inner continuity of life: this transfiguration of fact into patriotic value reduced grief to the barest minimum.

Indeed, even this bare minimum gleamed with a twilight of joy, like the reflected light of some universally agreed-upon, if one may say so, sanctified *Schadenfreude*. It was grey, and at no point possessed the inexhaustible darkness of pure, unmitigated pain!

To establish peace, one thing might have sufficed, one might think: simply allowing each person the right to catch up – to learn again, to mourn again, to weep, hour by hour, cause by cause, for the pain we had passed over.

For here – let us not deceive ourselves – is, for now, the only clearly apparent common ground. The others are attempts, suggestions – if they are anything at all…

. . . .

Primal Sound

[October 1919]

Back when I was at school, the phonograph had just been recently invented. In any case, it was the epicenter of public fascination, which may explain why our physics teacher, a man with a penchant for tinkering in all kinds of crafts projects, taught us how to assemble such a device from the most basic components. All we needed was as follows: A piece of flexible cardboard folded into a funnel, the narrow round opening of which was immediately sealed with a piece of impermeable paper of the kind used to seal jars of preserved fruit, thus creating a vibrating membrane, in the center of which, we inserted a bristle from a sturdy clothes brush, projecting vertically. Using just this small unit, one side of the mysterious machine was ready; the receiver and transmitter were fully prepared, and it now remained to create a recording cylinder which, by means of a small crank, could be pushed close to the recording stylus. I don't remember what we made it from; we just found some cylinder, which we covered, as best we could, with a thin layer of candle wax. The wax had barely cooled and solidified when, with impatience growing within us due to the urgent gluing & machinations, we pushed each other aside to test our creation. One can easily imagine what happened next. When someone spoke or sang into the bell, the stylus stuck in the parchment transmitted the sound waves to the receptive surface of the roll as it was slowly turned. If, immediately afterward, the busy pointer was allowed to retrace its own path (now fixed with varnish), the sound that had just been our very own trembled and wavered from the funnel, returning to us unsteadily, indescribably quiet and timid, occasionally faltering in places. The effect was always the most perfect. Our class was not exactly one of the quietest, and it was indeed a rare thing when we managed to achieve such a degree of silence together. The phenomenon remained astonishing, even truly shocking, from one moment to the next. We were, in a sense, being confronted with a new, infinitely delicate aspect of reality, from which something far superior to us children addressed us, yet in an unspeakably tentative and, as it were, pleading manner. At that time, and throughout the years, I thought that it was precisely this independent sound, extracted from us and preserved elsewhere, that would remain unforgettable to me. That it turned out differently is the reason for this account. It was not the sound from the funnel that lingered in my memory, as will be seen, but rather the symbols carved into the cylinder that remained much more peculiar to me.

Fourteen or fifteen years may have passed since those school days when this dawned on me one day. It was during my first sojourn in Paris. I was attending anatomy lectures at the École des Beaux-Arts with considerable enthusiasm. What seemed to appeal to me was not so much the complex network of muscles and tendons or the perfect arrangement of the internal organs, but rather the arid skeleton, whose restrained energy and elasticity had already become apparent to me in Leonardo's drawings. However much I puzzled over the structural whole, it was too much for me. My gaze kept returning to the skull, in which, so to speak, the utmost to which this calcareous element could still exert itself seemed to me to have been accomplished; as if it had been persuaded here, precisely, to exert itself significantly in a decisive service, to take something ultimately daring, albeit bound within its narrow confines, already once again operating without limits.

The enchantment exerted on me by this special enclosure, sealed from an utterly earthly space, finally went so far that I acquired a skull myself in order to pass many nocturnal hours with it. And, as always happens to me with such things, it was not only the moments of deliberate engagement that made this ambiguous object strangely familiar to me — rather, I undoubtedly owe my intimacy with it in part to the fleeting glance with which we involuntarily peruse and perceive our familiar surroundings, provided they have some connection with us. It was just such a glance that I suddenly checked & focused upon, precisely and attentively. In the often strangely vigilant & inviting light of the candle, the crown seam had just become strikingly visible to me, and I already knew what it reminded me of: one of those unforgettable marks etched into a small wax cylinder by the tip of a bristle!

And now I am unsure: is it merely a rhythmic peculiarity of my imagination that since then, often at long intervals of years, I have repeatedly felt the urge to take the leap from this similarity, which I perceived so suddenly at the time, to a whole series of unheard-of experiments? I confess immediately that I have always treated this desire, whenever it arose, with the strictest suspicion — if proof of this is needed, it lies in the fact that I have only now, more than a decade and a half later, decided to make a cautious disclosure. Nor do I have anything more to say in favor of my idea than its stubborn recurrence, which, without any connection to my other pursuits, has surprised me here & there, in the most diverse situations.

What is being repeatedly suggested in my mind? It is this:

The coronal suture of the skull (which would now have to be examined) has — let us assume — a certain resemblance to the densely coiled line that the stylus of a phonograph engraves into the rotating cylinder of the device. Now, what if this stylus were to be tricked and its return track to be guided along a path that did not originate from the graphic translation of a tone, but was something that existed in and of itself — well, let's just say it: the coronal suture, for example —: what would happen? A tone would have to arise, a sequence of tones, a piece of music...

Feelings — which ones? Disbelief, shyness, fear, awe —: yes, which of all the feelings possible here prevents me from suggesting a name for the primal sound that would come into being...

Putting this aside for a moment: what kind of lines, occurring somewhere, would it be possible to put to the test? Which contours might we like to draw to completion in this way, so to speak, in order to then experience the effect they would have in another realm of meaning?

* * *

During a period when I was busy studying Arabic poetry, in which the five senses seemed to play a more simultaneous and equal role, I first noticed how disparately and peculiarly the contemporary European poet makes use of these sources, of which almost only one, the sense of vision, is overburdened with the world, and constantly overwhelms us; how meager, in comparison, is the contribution made by the inattentive ear, not to mention the indifference of the other senses, which remain aloof and active only in their usefully limited spheres, with many interruptions. And yet the finished poem can only come into being on the condition that the world, attacked simultaneously by five levers, is perceived, under a certain aspect, on that supernatural plane that is precisely that of the poem.

A woman, to whom this was mentioned in a conversation, exclaimed that this wonderful, simultaneous ability and performance of all the senses was nothing other than presence of mind and the grace of love — and in so doing she (incidentally) provided her own testimony to the sublime reality of the poem. But this is precisely why the lover is in such great danger, because he is dependent on this interaction of his senses, which he knows only coalesce in that single intrepid core where, abandoning all breadth, they converge, & where nothing endures.

In expressing myself in this way, I already have before me the image that I utilized as a convenient aid whenever similar considerations occurred to me. If one imagines the entire realm of experience in the world, including those areas that are beyond our grasp, as a complete circle, it immediately becomes apparent how much larger the black sectors are, representing that which cannot be experienced, measured against the unevenly lighter sections where the senses are illuminated.

Now the lover finds himself suddenly standing in the middle of the circle, that is, where the familiar & the incomprehensible converge in a single point, becoming complete

& absolute possession, albeit with the abolition of all particularity. This dislocation would not serve the poet; he must retain the manifold details; he is compelled to use the sum of the sensory impressions in all their breadth, and so he must also aspire to extend each individual detail as far as possible, so that his heightened bliss can leap through the five gardens in one breath.

If the peril for the lover lies in the narrowness of his perspective, then the peril for the poet lies in becoming aware of the chasms that separate one order of sense awareness from another: indeed, they are vast & deep enough to sweep away most of the world — and who knows how many worlds — from our sight.

The question arises here as to whether the work of the researcher can significantly expand the extent of these sectors in the plane we have assumed. Whether the achievements of the microscope, the telescope, and so many other devices that shift the senses upward or downward, tend not to fall in a different stratum, since most of the gains thus obtained cannot be penetrated by the senses, & therefore cannot actually be "experienced."

It would be premature to assume that the artist who develops this (if one may call it that) five-fingered hand of his senses into an ever more active and spiritual tool is working most decisively on expanding the individual spheres of meaning, only that his demonstrative achievement, since it is ultimately impossible without the miracle, does not allow him to enter his personal territorial gains on the general map that has been revealed.

But if we now look for a means of establishing the urgently needed connection between these strangely separated spheres, what could be more promising than the attempt suggested in the opening pages of this memoir? If it is proposed once again here at the end, with the reticence already cited, the writer may be credited to some extent with having resisted the temptation to arbitrarily allow his imagination to run wild with the points raised here. For this reason, the task that had been "passed over" for so many years & had repeatedly come to the fore seemed to him to be both too limited and too explicit.

Soglio, on the Feast of the
Assumption of Mary, 1919

(Preface to a Reading from My Own Works)

[Hottingen Reading Circle, Zurich, October 27, 1919]

L.H.'s thoughtful invitation,
which I am now, at last, able to accept,
gives me occasion — after a very long pause —
to resume reading in public once more.

I thank you in advance for the fact that you Swiss wish to be the first to (once again) listen to me [read from my works].

When I, back then / it may have been ten years ago / gave up holding readings, it occurred under the impression that the poem ... always lays claim to a

too narrow, }} immediate
limited

unity to be read out to many without further ado.

If I were to resume presenting my work, I thought, it would have to be in the form of a speech — for a speech is, by its very nature, an act of communication from place to place —; whereas (it can't be helped) I will have to offer up certain poems which may well seem to you entirely without context, even reckless, unless you were – to preempt the worst – to impatiently receive them as a kind of *poésie de luxe*.

The question as to whether – especially in a time so urgently in need of counsel – a work of art that arises without conscious intention should ultimately be permitted, and whether in the end it might not be acknowledged as a kind of assistance, encouragement offered from the furthest, most remote distance, an affirmation with the coefficient of *infinity* –; this question I will not raise now. It would create an atmosphere of discussion between us; and that is not the atmosphere that this evening should engender.

Permit me to say only this:

It didn't take these dreadful years to compel me to ask whether such a creation is something for which one can justifiably be held accountable.

Even when I walked, nearly twenty years ago, beside Lev Tolstoy over the forget-me-not meadows of Yasnaya Polyana, I had already thoroughly made my decision.

And since then – I don't know how often –, at every turn in my path, I have had to question my own activity, to question it with gravity & rigor, to examine & harass myself whether I might indeed persist in it rightly and remain steadfast.

Who could presume to vouch for the future?

But to this day, the voice within that holds me to account has always answered in the affirmative.

*

The works I have the opportunity to share with you this evening have in some way come out of the conviction that it is a true and rightful task to reveal the breadth,
  the vastness
    indeed completeness of the world
      in distilled expressions.

For: yes! I hoped to develop the poem into such a testimony — that it might become capable of grasping every phenomenon
    not only the emotional aspect
alone
in a lyrical manner —:
  the animal,
    the plant,
      every process; —
        to portray *a thing*
in its own peculiar emotional-space.

Don't be misled by the fact that I often invoke images from the past. Even those things, too, that have come to pass, remain rooted in the present – within the fullness of becoming – if not grasped in terms of content, but intensity. And we, as members of a world which, producing motion upon motion, force upon force, seem to plunge inexorably toward the less and less visible – we are dependent on that superior visibility of the past, if we wish, by way of parable, to imagine the restrained splendor that still surrounds us today.

I won't overwhelm you with arguments. I promise to be measured.

The choice of texts to be read is not predetermined. Under the influence of your presence & participation, I intend to decide upon one poem or another.

Please therefore allow me, as the moment inclines me, to offer a few brief remarks – & thus, from time to time, creating a space where you may draw together in thought.

In all this, I do not feel so much like someone courting your approval – what I ask of you is this:

Let us, as far as it lies in our power, do everything for the genuine, honest unity of this hour!

The Testament

[April 24-30, 1921]

In order to understand his condition at the close of that winter, it is necessary to revisit the summer of 1914. The outbreak of that catastrophic war, which disfigured the world for the span of many lifetimes, prevented him from returning to that incomparable city, the place to which he owed the majority of his opportunities. What followed was an endless stretch of waiting in a country connected to him solely through language – though, having lived in various countries, he had so thoroughly subordinated this language to his innermost tasks that, for a while, he came to see it as the pure and autonomous substance forming the basis of his creative work & mode of thought.

The bond to that friend, upon whose special abilities he had pinned hopes of securing a doctor, occasionally so urgently needed, grew increasingly tenuous and had already been severed long before the day this man, wholly devoted to his profession, suddenly succumbed to exhaustion.

His sole attempt to resume his work – interrupted by the loss of his entire natural life – ended abruptly when he was conscripted into a military regiment, forcing him into a repugnant and utterly wasted period in the capital of the country that had dominion over him. Freed after many months from these idle obligations and returning to the place where he had been biding his time, he found himself lacking the inner clarity and freedom necessary for his ineffable work to thrive. He also resisted incorporating it in any way with the grim disasters of those agonizing years: at the very least, he felt compelled to excuse his inability in several letters, admitting he felt like a child, plagued by toothache, who refuses even to touch the objects most dear to him.

Finally, when the war had already degenerated into the diffuse chaos of revolutionary convulsions, and he had even managed to distance himself somewhat from this senselessness by translating Mallarmé, he accepted an invitation to give readings. He left behind the city — long since utterly intolerable — and his nearly public apartment, plagued by visits from strangers and casual acquaintances alike, to answer a desired summons to another country; one that, incidentally, had remained neutral and beneficial throughout the recent years' upheavals. Yet this was the very landscape through which he had frequently traveled before, coming from the southern regions, intentionally keeping the carriage curtains closed: something in his nature clashed with the stark, dramatic mountainous landscape that earlier generations had so celebrated. It was this country that now offered itself to him through that attentive calling as well as through the hospitality at the shores of one of its lakes.

Even his new residence, located beyond the borders he had once found unbearable, soon became little more than an extension of his prior waiting, though somewhat gentler. Relief came, yet the crucial conditions for the inner repose essential to his work were still lacking. His residences changed frequently. He found himself compelled to forge numerous new connections, some offering brief satisfaction. The attraction that his serious yet incomplete solitude occasionally exerted on others against his will (a longing persistently denied) also led him into strange circumstances requiring he share and communicate extensively, undermining the accumulation of inner reserves & fostering anxiety within his psyche, month after month.

Then, after more than eighteen months, at the onset of a new winter, when a return to the ill-fated land, a sickroom still rife with war's aftermath & woeful fates, seemed inevitable, — something entirely unforeseen occurred: A remote, ancient manor was offered to him where a quiet, taciturn housekeeper awaited. Barely settled in (on November 12), he sensed a surrounding benevolence & benefit surpassing his highest hopes.

The spacious, low-ceilinged study with its white paneling, large old tiled stove, and open fireplace appeared to have been waiting for *him*; everything necessary was provided day by day, no explanations required — outside the windows lay a quiet park. Softly blooming charmilles framed the spacious lawn on either side, alongside an unframed pond, whose unceasing fountain's soundscape, as it were, translated into the ear what was so fulfillingly still for the eyes. As autumn advanced, the park with its grand plane trees and an avenue of ancient chestnuts stretching into the open deepened the effect of the view. Without constraining the visual desires, meadows fell gently, defining the foreground, while wooded slopes rose beyond: though he cherished the plains, in these moments of contemplation, the boundary suited his inner landscape, nurturing the realm within him with each passing day.

As far as he could remember, he had never felt more natural and protected; not even in that old princely castle so vital to his life, cherished almost passionately until its monstrous walls, once seeming indestructible, were shattered to their bedrock by the blind ravages of war. That castle above the sea had been expansive; the power of the ages & the figures that lingered within it prepared countless challenges for the soul; it had to become acquainted with many superior things before it could remain itself.

Here, in this modest, easily surveyed noble residence, a humble past waited to be overcome. Rooms & corridors, long uninhabited in their original purpose, held a simple appeal for those who discerned them intelligently; few portraits possessed enough presence to dominate the imagination; the living predominated, and the objects, modest in nature, demanded no more than the involuntary overflow of his immediately receptive mind.

Could he, who had been rescued in this unexpected refuge, now begin to reconstruct his shattered being? One suspects so. Yet one might consider him even more fortunate when learning that just before shutting himself away in these new surroundings, he was granted two equally unexpected strokes of luck: the opportunity to revisit two famous places in different countries, both inextricably linked to the history of his past. One was that unique city to which he owed not only the entirety of his spiritual education, but also the revelation of the sufferings & fortunes of his character in a deeper, more perceptible way than even people of strong inner vision experienced at his age.

Above all: inexhaustible grace imbued him (a moment one might call miraculous and perfectly timed) with that prodigious turbulence which overwhelms a heart that, stirred by a new infatuation, decides to love…

Yes, this too.

Thus, when such convergence occurs for someone so favored and gifted, one feels assured leaving him to a life so magnificently endowed with solitude.

And yet the notes and draft letters, where the conclusion of that remarkable winter is recorded in fragments, reveal failure instead, a cruel, bewildering loss.

The writer (apparently retrospectively) compiled these loose pages under the title "*The Testament*," probably because these reflections on his peculiar fate express a will bound to remain his *last*, even if his heart still faced many years of challenges ahead.

The Testament

„Mais j'accuse surtout celui qui se
comporte
contre sa volonté"
Jean Moréas

"But I really blame the one who
acts
against his will."
Jean Moréas

(in April)

Spring, which arrived so early this year that the cardamom flowers have blossomed in the fields and dandelions have already faded into scattering yarrows, has never been favorable to reflection — its powers do not support contemplation. Nevertheless, after so many months lost to it, one must seek focus in the final phase of this blessed refuge.

As my relationship with my Beloved had calmed enough that I foresaw that I would be able to devote my undivided attention to myself for a while, a small building, which I mistook for a barn & paid no further mind, appeared at the edge of the park. It turned out to be an electric saw mill, now running nonstop for ten days, whirring and buzzing relentlessly. My silence is shattered. I realize that what I had planned cannot be completed as a last-minute rush, like a postponed school assignment that now weighs heavily on my conscience. The time for work is over. Now the saw holds court.

How precise the judgment is. Strange: I realize how much I have heard all this through my hearing — and now it has already been taken away from me. At night, when I wake up, or in the late evening (for one works long hours there in the saw mill & sometimes the noisy workday starts soon after five o'clock in the morning), that broad, pure auditory-realm I had taken to inhabit so long ago restores itself with indescribable gentleness. It was just beginning to be 'patterned,' as it were, by little birdcalls; but its center was still the fountain, and now I lie down in the middle of the night and bid it farewell. This was it, what should have provided me with the order I needed throughout these many following weeks of balanced, listening attentiveness. How I understood it immediately, how I absorbed it, on the very first day: this multifaceted variation in its flow. The slightest breeze changed it, and when it was completely still around the suddenly isolated jet, cascading upon itself, it sounded quite different from the noise it made in the mirrored surface of the water. Speak, I said to the fountain, & listened. Speak, I said, and my whole being obeyed it. Speak, you pure meeting of lightness and weight, you, the tree of games, you, a parable among the heavy trees of fatigue that fester within its cortex.

And with an involuntary & innocent cunning of my heart, so that nothing would be but this, from which I wanted to learn to be,

— I equated the fountain with the Beloved, the distant, restrained, silent one.

Ah, we had agreed that silence should reign between us: it would be the law of this winter, a harsh, implacable law — but now our tenderness was beginning, & not only ours; the weariness of what had been achieved would dwell in my heart. Perhaps — the necessity was so immense — we would be strong enough to keep silent, — but we would not have broken it; the mouth of fate opened & showered us with tidings. For love is the true climate of destiny; as far as it stretches its orbit through the heavens, its Milky Way of billions of stars of blood, the country beneath these heavens lies pregnant with calamities. Not even the gods, in the transformations of their passions, were powerful enough to free the earthly Beloved, the frightened and fleeing one, from the entanglements of this fertile soil.

Is what I am writing madness? Why do lovers' letters never address this conflict? Alas, their worries are different. It always seems as if the lover is swinging the Beloved higher than he could ever throw himself. Her desire for him makes him more beautiful and more capable. The expectation of her open arms inspires his race. His achievement clarifies itself in the contours of happiness, where otherwise it flowed over into the grim darkness of longing. Only now, at her heart, does work become stormy & sweet for the toiling man — and repose, infinite. Only now does the sediment of his boyhood nights dissolve the fear; only now does he see through to the depths of the night.

And if something disturbs their joy, it stems from obstacles, hindrances, or threats to this union; all distress & danger boil down to one worry: losing each other; and nowhere is there more doubt than in jealousy. But what about the one who already knew? The one whose heart was already filled with the loneliness of lovers. From early on, he knew the pure face of his Beloved. As he fled from the family resemblances that surrounded him, that constituted a claim on him, feature by feature, her face became his own future: through her eyes, he gazed into the Open. His little hand rested quietly in hers, which led him and never took possession. Growing up, he gradually became aware of her tall figure — at that time, she occasionally approached him & tested him like a javelin.

And later she threw him.

Ah, how could the lover surprise *him* who, more than a memory, became conscious of this: of this choice; the voluptuousness of the taut arm, the feeling of being thrown – oh, and the trembling as it hit its target.

And yet who would have so celebrated the lover, longed for and desired the Beloved, than this being used in a divine way, whose fate had already been decided!

It was as if, on the path he had traveled with the power of solitude, he had recognized the figure of his beloved in a more perfected way than anyone before him. And this knowledge, which was infinite, awakened infinite deprivation in him.

He fled from her, by calling her. Somehow, he was forced to submit to her, to endure her, to overcome her. For was there not a flaw in his drive that had to be completely justified, while he feared and avoided the one who demanded everything from him? Didn't this aversion of his feelings from her at the last moment falsify his sensitivity altogether? Wasn't this fear of being loved, which stemmed from the sufferings of his earliest childhood and never left him, a warning he had to submit to until the very end, or was it rather the fact that she was correcting the oldest of his misconceptions, to heal him?

Did a lover exist who would provide no obstacles, who would not slow him down or distract him with the matter of love? The one who would understand that he had been thrown far beyond her the moment he pierced her? Was there a blessed one who would consent to his great journey after being thrown, who wouldn't think of diverting him & keeping him surreptitiously, and who wouldn't rush forward to obstruct his path again and again? The one who had perhaps already been abandoned, who left it to chance how many more times he would be hurled through her, to the target, from the hand of his goddess?

Oh, if she existed, then he would be saved, just as he had, in other ways, when he arrived in Russia as a young man. The afflictions of his childhood had led him to assume until the end of his second decade that he lived entirely alone in the face of an adverse world, daily rebelling against the superior power of all. The injustice of such an attitude could only generate something deformed and pathological, even in the face of genuine emotions. Russia, not by slow persuasion, but overnight — literally: on the first night in Moscow — gently released him from the evil spell of this bias and embarrassment. Without boasting of it, effortlessly, as if through a pure season of the heart, the conciliatory country provided him with inexhaustible proof to the contrary. How he believed in it; how it delighted him to become fraternal. And even if he always remained a novice in professing this harmony (perhaps because he was not allowed to remain on Russian soil), he never forgot it; he knew it, he practiced it.

*

Certain emotions, strange ones, converged later into an image I loosely understood as that of a *revenant*. This experience denies me the right – or challenges my right – to be wholly immersed in the Beloved (no matter how vast or infinite the space she grants). I must acknowledge the law in this mastery, yet I feel simultaneously confined and self-willed. My deepest conscience torments me, not with the creaturely fear of sweet dissolution born from love's very core, but with the dread of apostasy that haunts me constantly, urging me to accept that I cannot govern my own desires: it is as if the capital of my emotions is divided, leaving me impoverished;

as if, though loved and loving, I am forced to take from a depleted reserve of emotion from unknown heirs already living off them. Somewhere in this vast emotional expanse, unease stirs — restlessness, resistance; unfathomable laments drift across my being, threats rise within me: I find no unity within myself any longer.

But this unity, inexplicable as it is, is the court before which I have stood since childhood. I exist within a realm where veiled judges pass sentence beneath hooded eyes —: I have never stepped outside it.

My life is a singular kind of love, already fulfilled. Just as loving St. George's eternal battle with the dragon, the expenditures of my heart have reached their culmination, transformed into a final event. Occasionally, I am lifted into this essence: an image of consummation.

(The princess, by contrast, occupies another place. She prays and awaits this moment. She kneels.)

Do not fool yourself, artist, into thinking that your proof lies solely in your work. You are not your persona, nor what others may assume you are out of ignorance, until this guise becomes so ingrained that it feels like second nature and you *cannot* do otherwise but exist within it. In this way, as you labor, you become the spear cast with mastery: laws take hold of you from the archer's hand and drive you into the mark. — What could be more certain than your trajectory?

But the real test, the real proof, is found in the times when you are not cast. When the archer, solitude, has long abandoned you, she forgets you. This is the moment of temptation, the moment of doubt, when you feel powerless, unfit. (As if remaining prepared weren't challenging enough!) Then, as you rest lightly, distractions take hold and seek other outlets — becoming a blind man's cane, a bar in a lattice, or a tightrope walker's balance pole. Or they root you in the soil of fate, so that the miracle of seasons might unfold within you, and you might sprout green leaves of joy…

So, bold one: rest heavily.

Be a spear. Be a spear. Be a spear!

This game of acceptance and refusal, where much is at stake, forms the very pastime of life for most people and fuels their drives.

Artists, however, are those who have renounced both gain and loss through an absolute and unwavering assent: for in their realm, neither exists as law or as pure obedience.

This final, free affirmation of the world elevates the heart to another level of experience. Its realms of choice no longer bear the names of happiness or unhappiness, nor do its poles bear the brands of life and death. Its measure cannot be found in the distance between opposites or the tension of antitheses.

Who still thinks that art represents beauty? That it has a counterpart? (This quaint notion of 'beauty' rooted in taste.) What drives it instead is a passion for the whole. Its result: equanimity and the balance of completeness.

?

If I did not resist the lover, it was because, among all the powers one can hold over another, hers alone, her unyielding power, appeared justified to me. Vulnerable and exposed as I was, I did not seek to *evade* her; yet I yearned to pierce her, to cross her boundary! Let it open a window onto the broader realm of existence… (not a mirror.)

This abrupt (what can I call it?) partiality in love stirs within me apprehensive recollections that surpass my own being: as if, at some point, I had experienced boundless impartiality...

Asceticism, of course, is not a true escape; it is sensuality with a negative connotation. It can serve as a temporary aid for the saint; at the midpoint of his renunciations, he perceives the God of conflict, the unseen God, whom he has yet to create.

But if his senses compel him to accept phenomena as pure & form as true on earth, how could he possibly begin with renunciation? And even if initially useful, it remains, for him, a deception, a ruse, subterfuge – ultimately, it will exact its revenge within the contours of his work – as severity, dryness, stubbornness, and fruitless cowardice.

Letters: how I was torn apart this winter; each letter a shock, an attack capable of overturning everything, or a profound invasion that altered the blood –

and this, daily, during what was meant to be the time of my purest equanimity.

And after nearly twenty years, with increasing clarity of will, I had shaped my life so that there was no longer, nor was there allowed to be, any news that could reach or change that will in its essential determinations.

My heart retains a strange, timid capacity for fear that renders it unrecognizable to me.

(From a draft of a letter)

Remember, Beloved, that all these refusals concern your power. If I were free, if my heart were not tethered like a fixed star within the bonds of an irrefutable spirit, then every word that fuels rebellion here would be refusal, denial, lamentation — your glory, turning toward You, consent, agreement — fall & resurrection in You.

If I were a man shaped by tangible surroundings, a merchant, a teacher of concrete things, a craftsman…

This contradicts the enigma of my life.

As the Beloved draws all events toward herself, I lose my authenticity; now, caught in the constant flow, even that which escapes my control seems to be drawn *toward* her. Partly, this stems from her will; partly, this possession arises simply from her mere existence. She has transformed the landscape within her lover's mind and dwells in its deepest recess —: the valley, where all things converge and vanish.

The saw has been running since dawn. My gaze, somehow surviving, still lingers wistfully on this seemingly intact environment, while the destruction unfolds relentlessly in my ear. It's often said that those who die do not lose all their senses at once. Their sense of taste is gone, touch dulled, hearing faded. But they can still see. Occasionally, if they have the strength, they turn their heads slowly on the pillow, letting their gaze wander across a new frame of images before them. Saying farewell with only *one* sense is a certain relief.

Without the interference of the saw mill over there, I would have held on to all this until the very end, though too late to benefit from it. I doubt I would have allowed myself the slow dawning realization I now experience day after day, while the jolt of departure finally brought me to confront the despair of what I left unfinished, plunging me into a dreadful fall, a terrible blow, like a solitary boulder. I don't know what might have become of me, but I fear the image of the Beloved within me would have been buried as if under a landslide.

Is this my progress, then? (I admit with some irony that I search for progress while weighed down by my conscience.) Is it progress that I painfully chisel away the stone above my Beloved's head that otherwise would have shattered her pure existence? (Where does the stone-dust drift? Who breathes it in? Guilt, surely, is not extinct.) Yet *she*, the Beloved, remains blameless. Perhaps this is also progress (as if I could only distance myself from loss by "stepping forward"!), even this, that I no longer call the divide between work and love a rupture; it opens *within* my love itself, for I have finally realized that my work is love. What an oversimplification! And now, as far as I can see, this is the only true conflict in my life. Everything else amounts to tasks.

I first became aware of it at military school; later, as an infantryman. And now once again: every creature bears only as much of *that* weight as its strength allows, even if it often surpasses it.

Yet *we*, positioned at an incomprehensible midpoint amid various and mutually conflicting environments, suddenly endure a weight entirely mismatched to our capacity & its use — a weight *strange* to us.

(When, for instance, would a swan be expected to face a trial meant for a lion? How could a bat comprehend a fragment of a fish's fate — or how could the snake, the digester, grasp the fright of a horse?)

I therefore believe that, since childhood, I have prayed only for my hardest fate, *my* own weight, not mistakenly that of the carpenter, coachman, or soldier, for within my hardest fate, I want to recognize myself.

It is only from the confusion inherent in the boundlessly human & the inquisitive in *all* things — which has allowed everything to happen to everyone — was it possible for destruction to fall into disrepute. How intimate it becomes when caught in what is most unique to oneself, in what one achieved with passion!

Nothing will remain of that "strange" affliction that led me one morning, at four o'clock, to the town of G. (still night, cold rain falling in the darkness), because here I began my work of knowledge and reflection. No one will ever know what I entrusted to these pages in silent reckoning. Before burning the small blue leather notebook I carried on my journey, I want to describe its state. Fewer than three pages are written in it, but what fills them, besides two addresses, makes the many empty pages so sinister I must cast them into the fire like contaminated, pestilential matter. Here I transcribe them without alteration, in sequence: the senseless words in which my then capable mind disintegrated when suddenly a "strange" weight, like corrosive acid, poured over it.

(From the destroyed notebook:)
(At the top margin, the word:) Nightmare—,
(then disordered numbers, small, meaningless additions, then:)

"silver joy rawness the surroundings fate Beloved
infusion sand why never attention
ambush down envy glutton prosperity vice
gnawer path branch immersed fence legend credulity
wasp heart cinema (child) mourning dewy
rumor ring gentleness night cradle
living food bird wheat-ear fate no
baptismal-font wrath turbidity multicolor applause
being mule corrosion far away fall-out
hairstyle fences typhoon oh cradle May
January silver mist paths call letter
messenger Busta note automobile Timgad shore
feed-rack drink novice nod oh axis
brightness finch helm storm stone Ribe
St. John's bonfire service August pose poseur
nun eddy spear rinsing lively
seam notch being exact burden hollow (?)
grip slaver claw exercise night-train zeal
desert spear frenzy break-in rage run
Lebzelt trembling-grass afternoon ubiquitous 100
cure yeast Wieburg spendthrift
king thorn step ungood unworthy gutter
keystone trill betrayal shame east Fehr
casein affliction crown bishopric berry
bier bear dwarf cicada seal bad

(New page:)

return loved one diver bird's head
cold sweat choker frost vikuña
ring-band trolley Liebknecht Agnese
Terwin yam guest role glasses will school
do-good Maria Iffland heartblood soul whimper
Zweibruck quitting-time Wendlandt descent
trace slope decline narrow pike fence-
guest Larde Feilitzsch drip determination
only bast roar ballast nightheart stubbornness
clean Urgast Billung prepared
seam-duress Niefeln Hieber encouragement
Icthüs nomenclature Beinung judge
ruler gallows military-power carding spool
plays slowly but no music comes
to the Naumann round dance"
(And three addresses.)

(Draft letter)

As long as things remain this way between us, I don't know how to live — because I'm incapable of doing so knowing that I am the cause of your unhappiness, just as much as I struggle when I try to make you happy *the* way you now expect. If only I had been utterly ruthless in that moment, striving for the freedom of my love! There is no greater prison than the fear of hurting a lover. It distorts every impulse of the heart; without it, I wouldn't have needed to plead for solitude in our happiness, as an exception. *My solitude* — this strange aspect of my existence — now appears as an escape from our love — and how could it not always be burdened by your desire, to prevent it from lingering too long? And then: how will you find the strength, once again, to stay away from my seclusion, which, beginning in our enclave of happiness, has an effect far beyond what was intended?

Should I consider myself forever doomed to unhappiness (ah, & worse still: as the cause of sorrow to the most blissful of hearts!) because I cannot so easily receive love just to derive from it the enhancement of my abilities?

I never thought much of those who lack the fire to ignite their spirit; why should I count on such motivation, when work itself is infinitely more love than any one person can summon from within themselves? It is *all* love.

And so this fervor for the Beloved appears to me like a unique kind of love, which doesn't spare or make anything easier — instead, because it remains unresolved, it demands the highest effort to be endured, understood, and fulfilled in all its demands.

Say it, say it — I speak what seems a strange burden to bear, an exception, perhaps a confusion of my own nature. Rarely has such a thing been lamented. Perhaps it is because most only focus on pleasure and jealousy, or because what remains to be endured in rare cases like mine falls into the realm of the unspeakable, the inexpressible.

There aren't many whose hearts, once thrown, don't end in an embrace; if they pursued it further, — they might see how its arc takes on a strange quickening beyond — that of impatience, as if it already wants to supersede this happiness. And beyond that, it stretches into the infinite, signifying — guess what? — the journey & longing of those who never stop moving — the Russian pilgrims and the Bedouin nomads, driven onward by their olive-wood staffs…

Only those meant to die within the embrace can truly find a home there; everyone picks their abode based on how they imagine their death (let me put it simply, with a bit of lightness). What drives those men out to the steppes, to the desert, wandering, is the feeling that dying at home just isn't welcome — they can't find their place there.

A Swedish friend, who spent a winter alone on the edge of the desert, wrote me:

> "...... Landscapes of such grandeur that there might be enough space after death. At least for a while —."

Despite everything, my God, how rich, how calm, how complete I would be now if this love had been granted to me unconditionally, free from the weight of hopes, expectations, and demands of that heart, which seems unable to possess its happiness precisely because of its profound fear of loss.

If only I had not feared it & had not been anxious when it lay ahead of me, unsuspecting — it might be here now, perhaps overcome (and yet no less present, for what could be transient in it!), perhaps always imminent…

The foundation of my work is a passionate submission to the object that holds my focus, the one to which, simply put, my love belongs.

The reversal of this submission occurs unexpectedly for me, in the creative act that suddenly arises within me, in which I act and overcome just as innocently as I was purely & innocently subject in that previous phase.

For a heart thriving within such circumstances, being in love might perhaps always be a fatal inevitability. It also yields, as is its nature, to the Beloved, not shaping them, but through infinite surrender, enticing them to assert control. The reversal, essentially the transformation of love into its Beloved — almost an opposition to itself — cannot fully counteract its own dominance…

Therefore, the experience of love appears as a kind of diminished, powerless subsidiary form of creativity, as its degradation — & left unrealized, untamed, & when measured against the higher order of this achievement, illicit.

Ah, I now live here as though I'll only remain in this place, which is known for its electric saw mill, for just a few weeks,

... without harboring any specific expectations for this stay, for which I am too exhausted to fulfill...

That solitude in which I have anchored myself for twenty years mustn't become a rare exception, a "holiday" I need to request from a state of watchful happiness with many justifications. I have to inhabit it, without boundaries. It must be the fundamental consciousness I can always return to, not expecting it to be fruitful, but arriving there involuntarily, unstressed, innocently: like the place where I truly belong.

What forces have conspired to converge within my heart?...

They recede upon discovering it is already inhabited.

Someone who, alas, can count being beloved and loving as nothing within the true conclusions of their heart.

?

How tired I am of launching these counter-strikes to defend myself against the powers of love –; where is the heart that would never 'demand' from me a specific, stubborn happiness, but instead would let me freely offer *that* which springs inexhaustibly from within?

Striving & resisting: I am exhausted by it. Where is the heart that never 'insisted' on a stubborn happiness, but allowed me to prepare for it *what* springs inexhaustibly from me?

Yet no consensus exists on this. Ah, if only the struggles would cease! If only we could hear, as in the final stanza of Girard de Roussillon:

> "Les guerres sont finies et les
> œuvres commencent."

> "The wars are over and the
> works begin."

Or Rimbaud:

To stir language with an impetuous heart until it becomes, if only briefly, divinely "use-less" — then move forward, never look back, become a merchant.

I knew all winter: I must meditate on something. Alas —, this is the most painful loss: to have lost something unknown, something impossible to decipher.

These days rank among the most difficult.... The aversion to what remains unfulfilled corrodes my body like rust; even sleep offers no relief —, half-awake, the blood pounds in my temples like heavy footsteps that refuse to rest.

If only I could call you..., but that would destroy my last refuge —: this court where I recognize myself. You recently wrote that I am not one who can be consoled by love. You were right. After all, what could be more useless to me than a life that allows itself to be consoled?

Oh, none of this took me by surprise as it might a madman in his delirium or a fool in his frenzy. While my judges pronounced the verdict with frustrating slowness beneath the light of my happiness, I stood beside them, witnessing the entire verdict unfold.

One night, however, I reached my limit. The protective silence of the house, which still supplies all necessities, and my shocking isolation within it, sparked a conflict in my heart so intense that I doubted I could continue living. Unable to read, or even find comfort in the ever-warming fire among the fir trees, I took down a folder from the bookshelf, one I had never opened before, and forced myself to examine its contents. The pages displayed reproductions of paintings from the great galleries, and their vague, disharmonious colors irritated me. I don't know how many images I fixed my gaze upon; there were countless ones, & I turned the pages ever more rapidly: suddenly, I realized what had been gnawing at me: Where to? Where to?

Where to, to freedom? Where to, to the calm of existence itself? Where to, to the innocence that had become indispensable?

I returned to myself; more alert, even wary, as if some inner awareness had burst forth,

I immersed myself in the open page. It was Jan van Eyck's so-called *Madonna of Lucca* — the gentle Madonna, wrapped in a red cloak, offering her delicate breast to the child, who suckles absentmindedly, body curled in.

Where to? Where to?......

Suddenly, with all the fervor my heart could summon, I wished not to be one of the two small apples — in the painting — nor one of those painted on the windowsill —: even that would be too much for my fate... No: my desire consumed me to become the gentle, humble, inconspicuous shadow of one of those apples —, that was the wish that engulfed my entire being.

And as if such a desire could be fulfilled, or was enough to secure a profound insight, tears of gratitude welled in my eyes.

Sometimes, amid the despair that relentlessly challenges me these days, I am surprised by something like the faint early glow of a renewed spiritual joy: as if, in truth, everything had become clearer and an ineffable fate was roughly apprehended. For isn't the essence of it (if I must express it so): that within my deepest self, light & darkness are not determined by the dominant influence of any person, but solely by something nameless. This, one might say, is the bare minimum of my piety: through renunciation, I should find my way back beyond the first crossroads of my life —, beyond its earliest, quietest, & freest decision. Beyond myself.

(Draft letter)

Castle B…, undated:
always.

To whom, Beloved, if not to you, should I entrust this difficult conclusion of my heart? If it causes you distress, then imagine the depth of the pain that compels me to write what follows.

I have committed an injustice; a betrayal. I failed to take hold of the opportunities that opened to me after six years of destruction and obstacles with B… the urgent inner task; it has been wrested from my hands by fate. I must now admit this to myself.

You know, dear, how much those circumstances, from the most accidental to the most essential, brought me joy, and how resolutely I gave myself over to them. You tried to preserve them for me: we didn't succeed.

On December 2nd, immediately after the fortunate attempt to draft that preface in French, I managed to sketch the first lines of the work meant to shape my renewed inner focus. By the fourth day, I was interrupted by the tiresome correspondence of my birthday, & on the sixth, troubling news arrived from G.

You know the rest; you know everything; there is nothing more to tell.

Do you see? All remained within my small miscarriage of December 2nd: the work, the life that filled me, withdrew with it.

At times there were glimpses of hope and joy, but they were followed by anguish and despair, — the tremors never ceased; you couldn't prevent them.

(What good did it do that I knew I could only be fulfilled and unsettled in my work!)

And even later, even now, even in these last weeks, I have not come to terms with my natural solitude — the only way to master myself. My heart has shifted from the center of its circles toward the periphery, where it was closest to you —, however vast, sensitive, jubilant, or fearful it may be there, — it is not within your constellation, not the heart of my existence.

In our sweetest & perhaps most just moments, beloved, you assured me you could hold all forms of love for me. Ah, steady yourself, ..., descend to the one who, whatever her name, sustains *my* life, and strengthens me as she can. I cannot escape myself. For if I were to abandon everything and blindly throw myself into your arms, as I sometimes long to do, and lose myself there —, then you would have someone who has given up on himself: you would not have me, not me.

I am incapable of masking or transforming myself. Just as in my childhood, facing my father's violent love, I kneel in the world and ask those who love me for mercy. Yes, spare me! Do not consume me for your own happiness, but help me nurture that deeper, lonelier joy within me, without whose grand proofs they would not have loved me in the end.

....

From the Literary Estate of Count C.W.

[At the end of November 1920/
end of March 1921

Schloß Berg am Irchel,
Switzerland]

FIRST PART

I

White horse — how? Or torrent's .. fall?
What image stayed behind in sleep's dim hall?
A chalice tilted, mirror-bright and deep —
Then day drove out the hush & hauled my sleep!

Returning — what within will I then meet,
when night lets fall its heavy inward feet?
Dream, now carry forth: is the plate of tin —
will the strange fruit reveal its skin?

Will I know what drink I truly sipped —, or
was it passion from a hill long dipped?
And whom to tell, when in the end decay
threads through the dregs that taste has
    drawn away?

Is it enough that outward still I gaze —,
Does sleep's cook still need herbs to spice
    his maze?
Or tosses he, with hesitant, unsure hand,
his seasonings into a dish unplanned?

II

Curtain, chessboard, and the slender handle
of that glass jug that betrayed the wine –
one late evening, later, knows the grandchild:
then his heart resolved it's way, it's line,

thus to go, as it must. But how?
Ah, toward women strangely did it fall.
(Dared he, even during mid-prayer, to allow
his gaze upon it…!) Without sense at all

it trembled before youthful faces! At times it took
its pace from some other man's command,
what urged it on was something vague, mistook,
and something vague as well would stay its hand.

Oft it started running through the sloping
of its landscape, like a child that flees,
further, further… till, in finger's pointing
–: stood there, breath-abundant, ill at ease.

III

Maiden, does summer's day make you bloom?
Evening holds quail-heartbeats in its warm room,
and the lover stands near.

He sees how your window frames you bright,
your posture held, your smile alight –
he senses you here.

The door is cool, and by morning light,
it will chill through and through.
But your friend burns hot. Oh, glow!
Glow, and draw him to you.

IV

That I should think of you beside the fire?
No, you are wrong — I read. — Ah, do you weep?
Can you still wish that I again aspire
to serve? For I did not love: I served in sleep.

You subdued in me what still, a boy,
was stubbornness and weakness, mute and raw;
with bleeding letters, not of joy,
I gave to you my very first year's awe —

Instead of riding, Olga, chasing game,
I knelt by you, while all the rest had gone
wrapped in silk that bore your gracious name,
a veil that from your mercy had been drawn.

Did you always sense that I was kneeling?
Or did you know: he does not meet my stare?
Ah, I was the shell, Aphrodite, & your own feeling
was the goddess — sea-born, riding there.

V

Let me softly leaf through your old pages,
great-great-aunt, foremother — let me try.
I don't know what phrase my thought engages.
Trouble, doubt, concern, and love, and lie —

all of that no longer weighs the same here.
Did you know how different we became?
Long since broke the favorite bench near
by the pond—and the wind, once sweet,
    the same...

Yours: because it knew how best to sever
loosened hair from off the blossom-ring —
left you, only just to reach you ever,
parted, shaped, and met you in the spring —

can it still be born from our own breezes?
Oh, spring presses round us, ever nearer.
Oh, to us, as well, the wind is danger — & the air
already is decision ... But *what* grew drearier?

Sorrow? — Aunt, ah yes, you surely bore it!
And you suffered well, you were not weak,
yet a moon there was, whose light unique
through the thickest fate still softly shone
    before it.

Roses tore into your dearest finger
with the thorn's short signature & sign —
illness, omen — none of them would linger,
each one walked the house with fate and

spine. Letters came, and even news would enter
like a shadow through the still delay;
children shaped their path to their adventure,
and the grown were made to *be* that way —;

all of this one barely dares to alter,
yes, you knew already of that stain,
that in lands abruptly led to falter
palaces would shatter once again —;

you thought at last you might have overcome,
when after many a year of bitter strain,
there still was something left, a little sum,
and harvest yielded tolerably again —

Even wildness bore its crown with meaning,
Paris rose from ruin new and wide —
lightly through the skies the balloon, gleaming,
(climbed as copper calendars implied)

many things rose fast, and faster tumbled —
and perhaps it's this that makes us reel:
that the spaces in between have crumbled.
Great-great-aunt! — if I could only feel

myself some nights like shepherds once,
    just staying
underneath this heaven overhead —,
down below the fields where sheep are straying —
(both you also trusted in, it's said)

stand and let it work in me, unknowing,
— whether it be meant for us or not —
and the stars within the Bear, far-glowing,
stretch my wakeful face into their knot.

Ah, but sometimes! I would enter, bright,
into the house again at morning's grey:
one with distance, for I reached in flight
beyond to you. The oldest trust held sway.

It cleared within my blood's inherited stream.
For tell me, what divides us from the whole
world, whether it should wander or should dream?
Here is November — yet the oranges

glow somewhere: what hinders me
from knowing them?

.... Halt. Now I will read

under your heart's heaven's line,
to move my quickened soul toward thine.

VI

Was the gust of wind just now
that blew sudden through my pane,
nature's rise and fall somehow –
blind and aimless once again?

Or did some decaying being
use that gesture to break through?
reach from soil, unseen, unseeing,
into where the house feels true?

Most times it's a nightly turning,
like a sleeper shifting sides –,
but then meaning starts its burning,
floods with fear that never hides.

Ah, I'm hardly trained or clever
to discern what it intends –
was it some boy, dimmed forever,
near me weeping through death's lens?

Does he (and I fail to follow!)
show what here he had to miss –?
With the wind came grief and hollow,
yet perhaps he stood and screamed this!

VII

In Karnak, it was. We had ridden in,
Hélène and I, after our hurried dine.
The dragoman drew rein: the Sphinxes' line –
ah, the great pylon! Never was I so aware

of a moonlit world! (Is it true you reveal
your greatness in me, already too much to bear?)
Is travel – seeking? Well, this was a goal.
The guardian at the gate gave first unease –

a terror of measure. How low he stood beside
the gate that ceaselessly strove to ascend.
And now, for the whole of our life, that column –
that single one! Was it not enough, its pride?

Ruin proved it right: the roof would bend,
too lofty it rose. Yet it endured, and bore
Egypt's night, unmoved forevermore.

The accompanying fellach withdrew.

We stood alone. We needed time to take
the strain of it – it nearly broke the thread –
that *such endurance* formed the very bed
of all we perish in. – Had I a son,

I'd send him there, the year he turns and knows,
when one breaks free and only truth bestows.

"There it is, Charles – go through the pylon, stand,
and look..."
For us it helped no more. But see –
to bear it was already much. You:
in your travel dress, worn through and true –
and I, the hermit of my theory!

Yet still – the grace! Remember still that lake
where granite cat-gods circled round the shore?
Marker – whose? And never was there more
enchantment in the form than in that make.

Had five not fallen from one side apart
(you turned around to see), their wordless pride,
stone-carved, feline, facing side by side,
would still hold court. And in that court, a heart

of judgment reigned. The pond's clear ban beside
the beetles at its edge – those giant forms –
and running down the walls, the epic storms
of kings in battle: all was judged. Yet tied

within that weight was mercy, strange and vast.
Each form with lunar clarity suffused,
each low relief with hollowed grace was used
as vessel ––: meant to hold, *and* so it passed

into containment what was never sealed,
never unread, yet veiled in such a way:
the world's deep secret, bare in its array,
was far too secret ever to be concealed!

Books leaf past it all: none ever saw
such open truth inside a printed page –
(what use to search a name, or make it law):
The boundless entered sacrifice's gauge.

– Oh see, what *is* possession, if it knows
not how to offer? Things must move along.
Let things go forth. Don't let a crack prolong
your soul's slow spilling. Rather let it flow –

be always giver. Mule and cow arrive
where, on his altar, stands the King's own face,
the god himself, like child at ease, in grace,
accepts, content. His shrine will still survive,

it never tires. It takes, and takes again,
yet gives such peace, such gentleness, such art,
the princess clasps the papyrus at its heart
but does not pluck it with a breaking pain. –

Here
all sacrificial paths are torn and lost.
The Sunday stirs, collects itself once more –

the weeks don't know what Sundays were before.
Man, beast haul gains aside at any cost,

spoils the god ignores or never crossed.
Commerce is hard, but still it can be done;
you train & train – the earth becomes less dear –
but he who *pays the price*, gives more than *one*.

VIII

Sometimes still I wholly feel that
childlike shout of *glee*:
when running down the hillside pastures
felt like destiny.

When to be beloved brought no burden,
no entangling care,
and the eye closed by the nightlight's flicker
like a flax-flower fair.

When to love was but a blind unfolding
of two arms in play –,
not yet circling One, or yet the Other:
~~(he is in danger.)~~
open, clear, and stray.

IX

What now again from purest logs so bright,
In chimney's heart flames up with fervent light,
Was once July, and August long ago –
Oh, how it burned within the wood's warm glow,
Entrapped, embraced, in timber's fiery flight!

If summer too had poured into our veins,
Our summer, when as grandest day remains,
Unveiling faces to the sky's expanse,
Revealing light that bids the soul to dance. –

They call it rising, victory from death –
yes, such a flame may well be what they meant;
for death was never set as counter-breath
to what here yielded, to the radiance bent

of this sun, and longed for it entire –
the heart matured, consoled, at last consents:
to die is: but the inward, reversed fire,
the burning deep within our "temperament." *

* *(Note by the copyist.) The word "temperament" is clearly the original word in the count's notes, but it seems that he was not satisfied with it; it is difficult to accept this word, which only refers to a way of applying our talents, in such a thoroughly typical sense. It was therefore crossed out and replaced with "elements," not without a certain regret, as one might surmise —, from the behavior of the hand.*

X

Strange the phrase: to while away the time!
To *hold* it fast – that were the greater trial.
For who is not afraid: where is remaining,
where *Being* stands, when all the rest is waning?

See, the day slows down toward that domain
which gathers it, when evening's shadow swims:
Rising has become a standing; standing, lying again,
and the willing rest already blurs and dims –

The mountains rest, with stars so richly crowned; –
yet even in them, time's faint shimmer gleams.
Ah, in my wild heart's night, without a bound,
Homeless abides eternity's gentle dreams.

SECOND PART

[Early Spring 1921
Schloß Berg am Irchel]

I

As though before the moving in, in vacant halls,
the woodpecker hammers at the bare elm's core;
above the roofs the winds stream, evermore,
with future plans, through airy walls.

This will one day be summer's sign,
a dwelling perfected, finished, whole.
What thronging presses at the door!
All enter blissful.
As if reward were granted.
Yet, what for?

II

Butterfly – what's hers, and what's mine,
Nature's and my own – how you unite!
Our shared joy, when on the trellised vine
You drift along like sketches made in flight.

Just before, I felt unmerited my station,
To partake in what the springtime gently frames;
For you can't fathom our soul's trepidation,
This heart, so burdened, lost in silent flames.

But now you've drawn my gaze's fragile thread
Into the April fabric, soft and brave,
And I do damage to the joy you spread
If still I struggle in the weaving stave.

III

New sun, with a wearied sense entwined,
yet mingled with surrender into joy;
but more than this, the shadow's new employ
of innocence takes hold upon my mind.

Shadows of earliest leaves you light to glow,
shadows of blossoms —: how clear!
How openly you stand, unmasked and near,
O year, that will not hide, nor feign, nor show.

Even our darkness softens by your art,
so pure perhaps was once its secret spring;
and once the ancient black of every smart
was young.

IV

You, whom I early learned already to revere,
did I divine you rightly, did I praise you true?
You holy one, you linger still in veils severe,
and only of your veils my blood once sang
& knew.

Though now and then to help compare,
Some tender, near-fulfilling came,
Yet still – she did not reach you there –
That was her final, whispered claim.

O proud, dark sorrow of my years
Of love! So let that be your name.
I held it up, like distant mirrors –
But never called it out in flame.

V

This morning first I saw the greying streak
that touched my temples, felt the mouth go stern.
You, who were still a child, if we should speak –
would now my heart be still the heart you'd yearn?

We walked once here along this path through grass,
beside the trellis where the bee-song rose.
And what now gently comforts me might pass
for grace, and speech for what no longer flows.

Would now my smile seem more paternal, dear,
just since it waited so, so long for you?
Would it seem strange? – Ah yes, it would appear
not like a friend from town would ever do.

Take it as landscape, I would say – don't turn
away just 'cause it towers over you –
. . . .
You, who were still a child – my long-lost year –
is that my triumph? Or what brought me low?

VI

To have endured all this – and joy as well,
endured it fully, deeply, and in peace – ,
soon came the test in silence, soon with speech:
who has not turned, amazed, from where they fell?

None ever mastered it; life persists
because none could ever master its twists.
Endless trials stretch beyond all time,
new beech leaves not so fresh, not so prime.

Since none can master, life stays pure.
Is it a quiet power that greets the dawn?
From that deep strength, the stone speaks soft,
and on that silent stone, the urn is closed aloft.

VII

O first bold cry flung level through the year –
the voices of the birds are held, unswayed.
But you already sound through time's frontier,
O cuckoo, fading into light and shade.

There – how you call, and call, and call, and call,
as one who sets the game but will not stay,
and build no song, my friend, no rise, no fall,
no cadence shaped the old remembered way.

We wait at first, and hope ... but strangely where
this cry goes cutting by,
it seems within this *Now* a Nevermore,
an earliest gone-by.

VIII

What kind of premonitions lay in sleep –
was it awe of joy and grief to be –
that even in your childhood letters deep
you always wrote the word "to Love" with a capital L,
Dorothee?

Even the ending flinched inside the word,
as though too bright a blaze might follow near.
Even: I'd love to… – that slight phrase you heard –
you forced in softest hand to show
a towering L, sincere.

That syllable lived in your heart apart,
always like a sentence still unspoken.
And before you dared to make it start,
your candles trembled from the fleeing
breath you breathed –
Dorothee –

IX

Lovely Aglaja, friend to all I feel,
our joy has reached the lark's ascending cry
high in the morning. Let us not conceal
our hearts from evening's chill beneath the sky.

Arc of our love – come, let us draw its line;
its rising shall be endlessly our praise.
And even later, when it does decline –: how fine,
how like your brow, so pure in its own ways.

Palermo 1862

X

I walked – it was I who sowed the fate,
and now it grows with joy, in full excess.
The bone lodged in the strangled throat lies straight,
as one with itself as in the fish's flesh.

I have no means to balance what I've done;
the weights tip heavy on the other side.
The sign still stands in heaven, touched by none –
it knows not yet how much in me has died.

For like the light of stars that wander far,
and reach us only once their source is gone,
our warped inscription at our vanished star
will first appear when we are long withdrawn.

XI

Often within glass-roofed nursery beds
another space appears, a mirrored gleam,
not this that breathed upon us like a dream,
but one to come, which memory instead

yields forth, yet never grants into our sight.
How narrow is the portion we are shown!
Who speaks the secret in the orange's stone?
Who reads the jewel by its inner light?

O music, music, say if you are able
to consummate the unheard hymn entire?
Yet you as well at last can only praise,
crowned air, for all you beautifully deny.

Letter to a Young Worker

[February 12–15, 1922]

Last Thursday, at a gathering, someone read from your poems, Mr. V., and the words have haunted me. I know no better response than to write to you — to set down, as best I can, what has remained unsettled in me.

The day after that reading, I ended up — by chance — in a Christian gathering, and that encounter may well have been the catalyst that ignited the flame that set this restlessness in motion & driven me to rush toward you with the entirety of my being. Beginning something requires a prodigious degree of force. I can't *begin.* I simply skip over what should serve as a beginning. Nothing is as strong as silence. If we weren't each born into the midst of speaking, silence would never have been broken.

Mr. V., I am not speaking of the evening when your poetry struck a chord in us. I'm speaking of the evening after. I feel compelled to ask: who — yes, there is no other way to put it — *who* is this Christ who keeps meddling in everything? He knows nothing about us — not about our work, our struggles, not about the joy we now fight to achieve, go through, & live — and yet, he still demands to be *first* in our lives. Or has that demand simply been placed in his mouth? What does he want from us? People say he wants to help us. Yet he acts strangely helpless around us. His world bore little resemblance to ours. Or do circumstances really not matter? If he were to step into this room now, or into the factory across the street — would everything shift, become whole, become right? Would my heart beat within me and, so to speak, continue on a different path, always in his direction? My gut tells me that he *cannot* come. That it would be pointless. Our world is not only outwardly different — it has no opening for him. He wouldn't *shine* through a ready-made coat; it isn't true, he wouldn't shine through. Wearing a seamless garment was no coincidence. And the core of light within him — whatever gave him that steady radiance — has long since dissolved, scattered into something else. But, if he truly was great, then, the least we could demand of him: that he somehow dissolved without a trace, indeed completely without a trace — without a trace...

I can't imagine that the *cross,* was ever meant to *remain* — it was only a station of the cross. It certainly shouldn't be imprinted on us everywhere like a cattle brand. It should be dissolved, even within him himself. For isn't it *so*: he simply wanted to create a higher tree, one under which we might ripen more fully. He, upon the cross, becomes this new tree in God, and we were meant to be the warm, joyful fruit that grows near the top.

Now, one shouldn't keep speaking of *that* which came *beforehand*; but rather, the *Afterwards* should have already begun. This tree, it seems to me, was meant to become one with us – or we with it, *upon* it – so deeply that we no longer need to concern ourselves with it, but simply and calmly with God, to whom he meant to raise us, more purely, more quietly.

When I say: God, I speak from a deep, never-learned conviction within me. The whole of creation seems to say this word – not without deliberation, but often from a place of deep thought. If this man Christ helped us to say it with a clearer voice, more fully, and more resonantly, all the better – but let him step aside. Don't always force us to relapse into the toil & tribulation it supposedly cost Him to "redeem" us, as people say. Let us, finally, enter into this redemption. – Otherwise, the Old Testament would even be better off – full of fingers pointing toward God, wherever one opens it, and someone always falls, weighted with himself, straight into the vortice of God. And once, I even tried to read the Qur'an. I didn't get very far, but I understood this much at least: such a commanding, pointing finger, and God stands at the end of its trajectory, in its eternal ascent — in an East that will never truly end. Christ certainly wanted the same: to point. But the people here have been like dogs, unable to understand the gesture, thinking instead they were meant to bite the hand. Instead of moving on from the crossroads, where the signpost had been erected high into the night of sacrifice, instead of continuing on from this Way of the Cross, Christianity has settled there and claims to dwell in Christ, even though there was no room in him, not even for his mother, nor for Mary Magdalene, as with every guide who points, who is a gesture, not a dwelling place. — And so, those stubborn in heart, those who keep recreating him and who live off the constant re-erection of crooked or overturned crosses — they do not dwell in Christ either. They are the ones responsible for the crowding, for the waiting and congestion at that one overcrowded place; they bear the blame for the halted movement, for the journey that no longer advances outward along the direction of the arms of the cross.

They have turned the Christian into an *métier*, a bourgeois occupation, *something static* – a pond alternately drained and refilled. Everything they do, by their irrepressible nature (if anything alive still stirs in them), stands in conflict with this remarkable disposition, and so they muddy their own waters and must continually replenish them. They burn with zeal to devalue the here and now – though we should meet this world with desire and trust – and by doing so, they increasingly surrender the earth to those who are willing to extract from it, as if from something spoiled and unworthy of better, at least a temporary and profitable advantage. Has this increasing exploitation of life not grown directly out of centuries spent devaluing the earth? What madness, to divert us toward an afterlife while we remain surrounded on all sides by tasks, expectations, and futures. What deceit, to steal images of earthly rapture and hawk them behind our backs to the heavens! Surely it is high time that the impoverished earth reclaims all the loans taken out on its happiness, loans used to embellish what is beyond. And does death really become more transparent through all the sources of light dragged in behind it? And doesn't everything taken from this world — since emptiness cannot sustain itself — end up being replaced by some deception? Are the cities filled with so much hideous artificial light and noise because the genuine radiance and song have been surrendered to a Jerusalem still to come? Christ may have been justified in speaking poorly of the earthly, given that his time was replete with stale and barren gods, yet still, (I cannot help but feel) this amounts to a kind of insult to God, when we fail to see, in what has been given and granted to us here, something fully capable — if used precisely — of enlivening us to the very limits of our senses. *Proper use — that's the key*. To take hold of the here & now, with heartfelt attention, with amazement, as our sole and provisional inheritance: *this* is, to say it plainly, the great instruction manual of God. Saint Francis of Assisi meant to write *it* down in his hymn to the sun, which, in his dying, appeared to him more glorious than the cross — the cross, which had stood only to *point toward* the sun. But by then the institution of the Church had meanwhile swelled into such a clamor of voices that the song of the dying man, drowned out in every quarter of the globe, heard only by a few simple monks, and infinitely affirmed by the landscape of his charming valley. How often must similar attempts have been made – to reconcile that Christian refusal with the evident friendliness and serenity of the earth. But elsewhere, even within the Church, indeed within its own crown, the locale culture pressed forward and forced its fullness and innate abundance into being. Why do we not praise the fact that the Church was robust enough not to collapse under the weight of certain popes, whose thrones were burdened with illegitimate children, courtesans, and the murdered? Was there not in them more Christianity than in the barren renovators of the Gospels – more, that is, of a living, irrepressible, transformed kind? We do not know, I mean, *what* will become of these great teachings; we must let them flow & be as they are, and not be frightened when they suddenly plunge into the jagged nature of life, churning underground into unrecognizable riverbeds.

I once worked in Marseille for a few months. It was a special time for me – and I owe it a great deal. Chance brought me together with a young painter, who remained a friend until his death. He was suffering from a lung disease and had just returned from Tunis at that time.

We spent a great deal of time together, and since the end of my appointment coincided with his return to Paris, we were able to spend a few days in Avignon. They remain emblazoned in me. Partly because of the city itself, its buildings and environs, but also because, during those days of uninterrupted and somehow heightened camaraderie, my friend shared with me many circumstances, with a kind of eloquence that seems, in certain moments, particular to the ill – especially when speaking of his *inner* life. Everything he said had a strange, prophetic power; through everything that surged forth in our often breathless conversations, one could glimpse, so to speak, the ground, the stones at the bottom – I mean to say: More than what belongs merely to us, it was nature itself, its oldest & hardest elements, which we brush against in so many places and upon which, in our most driven moments, we likely depend, as its slope determines our own inclination. An unexpected and happy love entered his life as well – his heart was unusually exalted for days, and so, on the other hand, the playful beam of his life shot up to remarkable heights. To experience an extraordinary city and a more-than-pleasing landscape with someone in such a state – that is a rare privilege; and so, looking back, those tender and at the same time passionate spring days seem to me the only true holidays I have ever known. The time itself was ridiculously brief – for someone else, it might have yielded only a handful of impressions – but for me, unaccustomed as I am to leisure, it seemed expansive. In fact, it hardly feels right to call it *time* – it was more a new state of freedom, a truly tangible *space*, a surrounding openness, not something transient. At that time, I was, if one can put it this way, catching up on childhood – and a part of early youth – for which, until then, I had never had the time or space to fully live out. I watched, I learned, I understood – and from those days also came the experience that saying "God" felt to me easy, truthful, and – as my friend might have put it – so carefree. How could that great house, erected by the popes, not strike me as overwhelming? I had the impression it could contain no interior space at all, but must have been built entirely of dense blocks of stone, layer upon layer, as if the exiles' only aim had been to heap the weight of the papacy – its preponderance – onto the scales of history. And this ecclesiastical palace truly does rise up over the ancient torso of a Heracles figure, immured into the rocky foundations — "Is it not," said Pierre, "as if it had grown monstrously from that single seed?" — That *this* might be Christianity, in one of its transformations, made far more sense to me than locating its power & taste in the increasingly weakened infusion of that *tisane*, which is claimed to have been prepared from its earliest, most tender leaves.

And are not the cathedrals, too, not the body of the spirit now declared to us as the true Christian essence? I could imagine beneath some of them the shattered figure of a Greek goddess lying in repose; so much blossoming, so much being has surged upward within them — even if, as if driven by a fear born of their epoch, they strove from that hidden body & reached into the heavens, which the tone of their great bells was charged with keeping perpetually open.

After my return from Avignon I went to church often — in the evenings, & on Sundays — at first alone... then later...

I have a Beloved — almost still a child — who works from home, and when the work is scarce, she often finds herself in truly dire straits. She's skilled; she could easily find work in a factory, but she fears the patron.

Her conception of freedom is limitless. It won't surprise you to hear that she also experiences God as a kind of patron, indeed as the 'arch-patron,' as she once said to me, laughing, but with a kind of dread in her eyes. It took a long time before she agreed to come with me one evening to Saint-Eustache, where I liked to go for the music of the May devotions. Once, we got as far as Meaux together & looked at tombstones in the church there. Gradually she began to notice that in churches, God leaves you in peace, that he makes no demands; one might almost think he's not present at all – don't you agree? – but yet, at the very moment when you are about to say that, Marthe added that, even if he's not there, something still holds you back. Perhaps it's nothing more than what human beings have instilled into that high, strangely fortified atmosphere over so many centuries. Or perhaps it's simply that the vibration of the powerful & tender music can never fully escape – indeed, it must have penetrated the stones long ago, and these pillars & vaults must be strangely agitated, stones – and even though stone is hard and difficult to access, it is ultimately shaken by the constant singing, by the repeated attacks from the organ, these assaults, the storms of song, every Sunday, these hurricanes of the great feast days. Calm — that is what truly reigns in the old churches. I said it to Marthe: Calm. We listened, and she understood it immediately — she has a wonderfully receptive nature. Since then, we would sometimes step inside wherever we heard singing, and we stood there, close together, listening. Most beautiful of all was when we could see a stained-glass window, one of those old narrative windows, with many sections, each dense with figures — tall people, small towers, and all sorts of events. Nothing was too strange for it — you see castles & battles and a hunt, and the white stag always appears again, in deep red and burning blue. I once drank a very old wine. That's what it's like for the eyes, those windows — only the wine was dark red on the tongue, whereas this contains, too, the blue and the violet and the green. In the old churches, *everything* appears boldly — not like in the new ones, where only, so to speak, the good examples are allowed to appear. Here, too, is what is cruel and wicked and terrifying; the crippled, the desperate, the ugly & unjust — and one wants to say that it is also loved, somehow, for God's sake. Here is the angel that does not exist, & the devil that does not exist;

and the human being who does exist stands between them, and I cannot help it — their unreality makes the human more real to me. I am better able to gather together what I feel when the word "human" is spoken inside one of those spaces, than out on the street among people who carry nothing recognizably human about them. But that is difficult to say. And what I want to say now is harder still. When it comes to the "patron," and to power (this became clear to me gradually, in there, when we were completely immersed in the music), there is only *one* way to resist it: by going further than it can go. What I mean is this: one should make the effort, in every instance of power that lays claim to authority over us, to recognize all power at once — power as such, the whole of it, the power of God. One should tell oneself: there is only *one*, and this lesser, false, flawed one is to be understood *as if it* were the very one that rightfully seizes us. Wouldn't that render it harmless? If in every form of power, even in the cruel and malicious, one were to see power itself — I mean *that* which ultimately has the right to be called powerful — wouldn't that allow one to withstand even the illegitimate & arbitrary, and remain unscathed? Don't we respond in just this way toward all unknown, great forces? We encounter none in their purity. We accept each one with its flaws, flaws that may correspond to our own. —And haven't all scholars, explorers, inventors, through the assumption that they were dealing with great forces, suddenly find themselves confronted with the greatest? I am young, and much rebellion still stirs in me; I cannot guarantee that I act according to this insight in every case when impatience and resistance overtake me — but in my deepest self I know that submission leads further than defiance; it brings shame to every power that merely wishes to possess, and it contributes — indescribably — to the glorification of true power. The one who rebels breaks away from the attraction of a center of force, and perhaps he even succeeds in leaving that force field behind — but beyond it, he stands in a void, and must look around for another gravitation that will take him in. And this second gravity is often even less lawful than the first. Why, then, not see the greater force in the one we already find ourselves within — undisturbed by its flaws and fluctuations? At some point, arbitrariness touches the boundary of law of its own accord, and we save our strength by letting it convert itself. Admittedly, this belongs to the slow, elongated processes that stand in stark contrast to the remarkable precipitousness of our time. But even amid the fastest movements, slow ones continue – some so slow, in fact, that their course lies beyond our own lifespan. And for that, does humanity not exist? To hold open the waiting for what exceeds the individual. – Seen from that perspective, the slow often proves to be the swiftest – meaning, it becomes clear that we only called it slow because it was immeasurable.

Now, it seems to me, there exists something wholly immeasurable – and still, people never tire of tampering with standards, measurements, and institutions. And this is most visible in that form of love they have defamed with an intolerable mixture of contempt, lust, and curiosity – the one they call "sensual." Here lie, perhaps, the most damaging effects of the degradation that Christianity felt it had to inflict on earthly things. Here, everything is disfigurement and repression – and yet it is from this most profound event, that we emerge, and within it that we again find the very basis of our ecstasies. It is increasingly incomprehensible to me, if I may say so, how a doctrine that condemns us precisely *there* where all of creation experiences its deepest bliss should still continue with such persistence, even if it proves itself nowhere, yet still everywhere asserts itself with such consistency.

Here, too, I think again of the intense conversations I was allowed to have with my deceased friend — then, in the meadows of the Île de la Barthelasse in spring, and later. Indeed, even in the night preceding his death (he died the following afternoon, shortly after five o'clock), he opened to me, out of a space of the deepest suffering, such pure vistas that my own life seemed, in a thousand places, to begin anew — and when I wanted to answer, no voice came. I had not known that there are tears of joy. I wept my first — inexperienced tears — into the hands of one who by morning would be dead, and I felt how, in Pierre, the tide of life surged one last time within him and overflowed as my warm teardrops joined it. Am I being effusive? But I am speaking of an *excess*.

Why I ask you, Mr. V., if help is what is promised us — to us who so often find ourselves helpless — why are we abandoned there, at the very roots of all experience? Anyone who would assist us *there* could rest assured that we would demand nothing more of them. For the succor he would instill in us there would grow of its own accord and become greater and stronger at the same time as our life. It would never run out. And yet how much is placed into our innermost secret being without care? How we must skulk around it – and finally stumble into our own beautiful sexuality like burglars or thieves, wandering, colliding, staggering within it, only to burst out again like convicted trespassers, into the twilight of Christian decency. Why, if guilt or sin had to be invented to account for the tensions of the inner life, why was it attached to this part of the body? Why was it allowed to fall there, into that region – left to dissolve into the clear spring at the center of us, poisoning and muddying it? Why was our sexuality made homeless, instead of making it the site of our rightful celebration, a festivity?

Fine, I'll concede, perhaps it's not meant to belong to us at all, we who are incapable of bearing or managing such inexhaustible bliss. But then why, from *this* very place, do we not already belong to God?

A churchgoer would surely point out to me that marriage exists – though he is not unaware of the state of that institution. It's not use setting the will to procreate under the glow of divine grace – my sexuality is not only directed toward offspring, it is the secret of my own life – and only because it, supposedly, must not occupy the central place there, so many have pushed it to the margins and thereby lost their balance. What good is all this! The dreadful untruth and insecurity of our time has its root in the unacknowledged happiness of the sexual – in this peculiarly skewed sense of guilt that continually increases and severs us from the rest of nature, even from the child, although – as I learned on that unforgettable night – its innocence does not consist in some supposed ignorance of sex – "rather," Pierre said, almost tonelessly, "that incomprehensible joy that awakens in us in *that* place, in the flesh of the closed embrace, is still diffused namelessly throughout the child's entire body." To describe the peculiar state of our sensuality, one would have to be allowed to say: Once we were child *everywhere* – now, we are so only in one place. – But if there is only one among us who is certain of this and who has the ability to show the evidence for it, why do we allow generation after generation to come to their senses under the rubble of Christian prejudices and stir like a half-dead person in darkness, in a narrow gap closed in by nothing but denials?

Mr. V., I keep writing and writing. A whole night has nearly passed in doing so. I must collect myself. – Did I mention that I work in a factory? I work in the typing room, but sometimes I also have to operate a machine. I once studied for a short time. In any case, I only want to say how I feel. I want, you see, to be of use to God, just as I am; what I do here, my work, I want to keep doing, toward Him – without my stream being broken, if I may put it that way, not even in Christ, who once was life-giving water to many. I cannot, for example, explain my machine to him, for he retains nothing. I know you won't laugh if I put it so plainly – it's best that way. But God – I have this sense – to *him* I can bring those things, my machine, & its first product, or all of my labor, it flows into him, without resistance. Just as once, it was easy for the shepherds to offer the gods of their lives a lamb, or the crops of the field, or the finest cluster of grapes.

You see, Mr. V., I was able to write this long letter without once needing the word "faith." For that, to me, seems a cumbersome and difficult matter – and not mine. I don't want to be maligned on Christ's behalf, I want to be good – for God. I don't wish to be addressed as a sinner from the start – perhaps I am not one. I have such pure mornings! I could speak with God – I need no one to help me compose letters to Him.

I know your poems only from that reading the other evening. I own very few books, mostly related to my work. A few, though, are about art, & some history, or whatever I've managed to get hold of. – Your poems, however – and now you'll have to accept this – have stirred this whole movement within me. My friend once said: Give us teachers who praise the here and now. You *are* one of these.

Original Sources

"Entwurf einer politischen Rede" (Draft of a Political Speech) (written 1919) was first published posthumously in *Aufsätze und Rezensionen* and later included in Vol. VI of the critical edition *Sämtliche Werke* (1955–1966). It remained unpublished during Rilke's lifetime.

"Ur-Geräusch" (Primal Sound). First published in: *Das Inselschiff.* Year 1, Vol. 1 (Oct. 1919) 14–20.

"(Vorrede zu einer Vorlesung aus eigenen Werken)" (Preface to a Reading from My Own Works). Source: Rainer Maria Rilke: *Sämtliche Werke.* Vol. 1–6, Vol. 6 (Wiesbaden & Frankfurt am Main, 1955–1966) 1095–1099.

Das Testament (The Testament), written April 24-30, 1921. First published as: Rainer Maria Rilke, *Das Testament* (Frankfurt am Main: Insel Verlag, 1974).

Rilke's original hand-written manuscript was also consulted, resulting in some deviations from the printed German version, which in parts did not conform to the manuscript. We have eliminated the editorial insertions of brackets made by the German editor and included Rilke's own question marks, slashes, cross outs (see pp. 48, 64, and 70), underlining, etc., sustaining his typographic symbols where sensible. That this was only ever a private manuscript Rilke did not publish is made more evident through our inclusion of his markings, particularly his use of cross-outs, strikethroughs, & question marks to denote passages he was deliberating whether to include or not. Our aim was to make clear the workman-like aspect of this text (the writer's infernal workshop), yet without being decorative, or making the book potentially illegible. These gestures of Rilke's own hand were copied from the original manuscript, which can be viewed here:

`https://www.e-manuscripta.ch/snl/doi/10.7891/e-manuscripta-52069`

Aus dem Nachlaß des Grafen C.W.: Ein Gedichtkreis. Aus Rainer Maria Rilkes Nachlass — Erste Folge Rainer Maria Rilke (Frankfurt am Main: Insel Verlag, 1950). ("From the Literary Estate of Count C.W."). Written November 1920 & April 1921, but not published until after Rilke's death.

"Der Brief des jungen Arbeiters" ("Letter to a Young Worker") was written February 12–15, 1922. First published in: Rainer Maria Rilke, *Über Gott. Zwei Briefe* (Leipzig: Insel-Verlag, 1933).

The following pages contain passages, lines, or markings from Rilke's original manuscripts: Opening spread, title page, 35, 36, 48, 64, 70, 84, 90, 91, 95, 96, 99.

About the Editor

Rainer J. Hanshe is a writer and the founder of Contra Mundum Press and the journal *Hyperion: On the Future of Aesthetics*. He is the author of two novels, *The Acolytes* (2010) and *The Abdication* (2012), and the editor of Richard Foreman's *Plays with Films* (2013) and Wordsworth's *Fragments* (2014). He is also the author of the hybrid entity *Shattering the Muses* (2016), *Closing Melodies* (2023), a phantomatic encounter between Nietzsche and Van Gogh, *Dionysos Speed* (2024), and *Humanimality* (2025). Work of his has appeared in *Po&sie, Sinn und Form, Asymptote, ChrisMarker.org*, and elsewhere. In 2016, Petite Plaisance published an Italian translation of his second novel, *The Abdication*. Shorter and longer works of his have been translated into other languages, and in 2021, the journal *Po&sie* staged an event at Maison de la poésie in Paris to honor his work. His own translations include Baudelaire's *My Heart Laid Bare* (2017; 2020), *Belgium Stripped Bare* (2019), and *Paris Spleen* (2021), Évelyne Grossman's *The Creativity of the Crisis* (2023), Antonin Artaud's *Journey to Mexico: Revolutionary Messages* (2024), and Léon-Paul Fargue's *High Solitude* (2024), as well as longer and shorter works by other authors. Eris Press published his translation of Fargue's *The Stroller of Paris* in 2025. *Beyond Sense*, a vatic exploration of the aphasiac disintegration of Hölderlin, Baudelaire, Nietzsche, and Artaud, is due out in 2026, *The Accumulating Wreckage* in 2027, and *Paris Without End: Assorted Translations From Giacometti to Artaud* in 2028. He is at work on a new book entitled *Burn Poet Burn*. Author site: `literaryabsolute.com`

About the Translator

Mark Kanak is a German-American writer, translator, and radioplay producer/creator, writing in German and English (simultaneously). He has published nine books and countless translations, including Walter Serner's *Last Loosening* (2020) and *The Tigress* (2025), Rolf-Dieter Brinkmann's only novel, *No One Knows More* (2022), Blixa Bargeld's *Europa Crosswise* (2022), and many others. He has worked in an editorial capacity for magazines (*perspektive*), produced radioplays, and provided contributions to many anthologies and journals (*Triëdere*, *IDIOME*, etc.). He is author of *Tractatus illogico-insanus* (2018) and *Lügendetektor/Lie Detector* (2023). His most recent radioplays include *Tollhaus* (Madhouse, 2022) *& Atmung* (Breathing, 2024), published by Belleville Verlag (Munich) and both featuring Blixa Bargeld of Einstürzende Neubauten in the lead role. Both were shortlisted for radioplay of the year by *Preis der deutschen Schallplattenkritik*. He also produces music under the name of "Irrflug," and his album "Silver" is upcoming as a vinyl release in Sähkö Recordings. *Tollhaus* will premiere as a film, directed by Sarah Earheart and Thomas Antonic, in 2026.

COLOPHON

THE TESTAMENT (& OTHER TEXTS)
was handset in InDesign CC.

The display font is *Albertus.*

The text font is *Diotima.*

Diotima was designed by Gudrun Zapf von Hesse in the late 1930s. Named after the ancient Greek philosopher Diotima of Mantinea, its roots lay in a calligraphic sheet of Zapf von Hesse's. One of its earliest uses was for Friedrich Hölderlin's "Hyperion to Diotima." D. Stempel AG first cast the metal typeface between 1951 & 1953, with its italic version added in 1950.

Book design & typesetting: Alessandro Segalini

Cover design: CMP

OPENING IMAGE: Rainer Maria Rilke: *Das Testament.* s.l., s.d.. Schweizerische Nationalbibliothek (NB), SLA-RMR-Ms_D_1, https://doi.org/10.7891/e-manuscripta-52069 / ⓔ

CLOSING IMAGE: Jan van Eyck, *Lucca Madonna*, 1436.

THE TESTAMENT (& OTHER TEXTS)
is published by Contra Mundum Press.

Contra Mundum Press New York · London · Melbourne

CONTRA MUNDUM PRESS

Dedicated to the value & the indispensable importance of the individual voice, to works that test the boundaries of thought & experience.

The primary aim of Contra Mundum is to publish translations of writers who in their use of form and style are *à rebours*, or who deviate significantly from more programmatic & spurious forms of experimentation. Such writing attests to the volatile nature of modernism. Our preference is for works that have not yet been translated into English, are out of print, or are poorly translated, for writers whose thinking & æsthetics are in opposition to timely or mainstream currents of thought, value systems, or moralities. We also reprint obscure and out-of-print works we consider significant but which have been forgotten, neglected, or overshadowed.

There are many works of fundamental significance to *Weltliteratur* (*& Weltkultur*) that still remain in relative oblivion, works that alter and disrupt standard circuits of thought — these warrant being encountered by the world at large. It is our aim to render them more visible.

For the complete list of forthcoming publications, please visit our website. To be added to our mailing list, send your name and email address to: info@contramundum.net

Contra Mundum Press
P.O. Box 1326
New York, NY 10276
USA

OTHER CONTRA MUNDUM PRESS TITLES

2012 *Gilgamesh*
Ghérasim Luca, *Self-Shadowing Prey*
Rainer J. Hanshe, *The Abdication*
Walter Jackson Bate, *Negative Capability*
Miklós Szentkuthy, *Marginalia on Casanova*
Fernando Pessoa, *Philosophical Essays*
2013 Elio Petri, *Writings on Cinema & Life*
Friedrich Nietzsche, *The Greek Music Drama*
Richard Foreman, *Plays with Films*
Louis-Auguste Blanqui, *Eternity by the Stars*
Miklós Szentkuthy, *Towards the One & Only Metaphor*
Josef Winkler, *When the Time Comes*
2014 William Wordsworth, *Fragments*
Josef Winkler, *Natura Morta*
Fernando Pessoa, *The Transformation Book*
Emilio Villa, *The Selected Poetry of Emilio Villa*
Robert Kelly, *A Voice Full of Cities*
Pier Paolo Pasolini, *The Divine Mimesis*
Miklós Szentkuthy, *Prae, Vol. 1*
2015 Federico Fellini, *Making a Film*
Robert Musil, *Thought Flights*
Sándor Tar, *Our Street*
Lorand Gaspar, *Earth Absolute*
Josef Winkler, *The Graveyard of Bitter Oranges*
Ferit Edgü, *Noone*
Jean-Jacques Rousseau, *Narcissus*
Ahmad Shamlu, *Born Upon the Dark Spear*
2016 Jean-Luc Godard, *Phrases*
Otto Dix, *Letters, Vol. 1*
Maura Del Serra, *Ladder of Oaths*
Pierre Senges, *The Major Refutation*
Charles Baudelaire, *My Heart Laid Bare & Other Texts*
2017 Joseph Kessel, *Army of Shadows*
Rainer J. Hanshe & Federico Gori, *Shattering the Muses*
Gérard Depardieu, *Innocent*
Claude Mouchard, *Entangled — Papers! — Notes*
2018 Miklós Szentkuthy, *Black Renaissance*
Adonis & Pierre Joris, *Conversations in the Pyrenees*

2019 Charles Baudelaire, *Belgium Stripped Bare*
Robert Musil, *Unions*
Iceberg Slim, *Night Train to Sugar Hill*
Marquis de Sade, *Aline & Valcour*
2020 *A City Full of Voices: Essays on the Work of Robert Kelly*
Rédoine Faïd, *Outlaw*
Carmelo Bene, *I Appeared to the Madonna*
Paul Celan, *Microliths They Are, Little Stones*
Zsuzsa Selyem, *It's Raining in Moscow*
Bérengère Viennot, *Trumpspeak*
Robert Musil, *Theater Symptoms*
Miklós Szentkuthy, *Chapter on Love*
2021 Charles Baudelaire, *Paris Spleen*
Marguerite Duras, *The Darkroom*
Andrew Dickos, *Honor Among Thieves*
Pierre Senges, *Ahab (Sequels)*
Carmelo Bene, *Our Lady of the Turks*
2022 Fernando Pessoa, *Writings on Art & Poetical Theory*
Miklós Szentkuthy, *Prae, Vol. 2*
Blixa Bargeld, *Europe Crosswise: A Litany*
Pierre Joris, *Always the Many, Never the One*
Robert Musil, *Literature & Politics*
2023 Pierre Joris, *Interglacial Narrows*
Gabriele Tinti, *Bleedings — Incipit Tragœdia*
Évelyne Grossman, *The Creativity of the Crisis*
Rainer J. Hanshe, *Closing Melodies*
Kari Hukkila, *One Thousand & One*
2024 Antonin Artaud, *Journey to Mexico*
Rainer J. Hanshe, *Dionysos Speed*
Amina Saïd, *Walking the Earth*
Léon-Paul Fargue, *High Solitude*
Gabor Schein, *Beyond the Cordons*
Marquis de Sade, *Stories, Tales, & Fables*
2025 Sara Whym, *Dreamscapes I — Betrayals (101 & 202 Nights)*
Tahar Bekri, *The Desert at Dusk*
Robert Kelly, *Listening Through*
Rainer J. Hanshe, *Humanimality*

SOME FORTHCOMING TITLES

E.M. Cioran, *The Book of Deceptions*
Isidore Isou, *The Making of a Messiah*

AGRODOLCE SERIES

2020 Dejan Lukić, *The Oyster*
2022 Ugo Tognazzi, *The Injester*

HYPERION *On the Future of Æsthetics* 2006–PRESENT

To read samples and order current & back issues of *Hyperion*, visit contramundumpress.com/hyperion
Edited by Rainer J. Hanshe & Erika Mihálycsa (2014 ~)

CONTRA MUNDUM PRESS

is published by Rainer J. Hanshe
Typography & Design: Alessandro Segalini
Publicity & Marketing: Alexandra Gold
Ebook Design: Carlie R. Houser

THE FUTURE OF KULCHUR

THE PROJECT

From major museums like the MoMA to art house cinemas such as Film Forum, cultural organizations do not sustain themselves from sales alone, but from subscriptions, donations, benefactors, and grants.

Since benefactors of Peggy Guggenheim's stature are rare to come by, and receiving large grants from major funding bodies is an infrequent and unreliable source of capital, we seek to further our venture through a form of modest support that is within everyone's reach.

Although esteemed, Contra Mundum is an independent boutique press with modest profit margins. In not having university, state, or institutional backing, other forms of sustenance are required to move us into the future.

Additionally, in the past decade, the reduction of the purchasing budgets across the nation of both public and private libraries has had a severe impact upon publishers, leading to significant decreases in sales, thereby necessitating the creation of alternative means of subsistence.

Because many of our books are translations, our desire for proper remuneration is a persistent point of concern. Even when translators receive grants for book projects, the amount is often insufficient to compensate for their efforts, and royalties, which trickle in slowly over years, are not a reliable source of compensation.

WHAT WILL BE DONE

With your participation we seek to offer writers and translators greater compensation for their work, and in a more expeditious manner.

Additionally, funds will be used to pay for translation rights, basic operating expenses of the press, and to represent our writers and translators at book fairs.

If the means exist, we will also create a translation residency, providing opportunities to both junior and more established translators, thereby furthering our cultural efforts.

Through a greater collective and the cultural commons of the world, we can band together to create this constellation and together function as a patron for the writers and artists published by CMP. We hope you will join us in this partnership.

Your patronage is an expression of your confidence and belief in visionary literary work that would otherwise be exiled from the Anglophone world. With bookstores and presses around the world struggling to survive, and many even closing, joining the Future of Kulchur allows you to be a part of an active force that forms a continuous & stable foundation which safeguards the longevity of Contra Mundum Press.

Endowed by your support, we can expand our poetics of hospitality by continuing to publish works from many different languages and reflect, welcome, and embrace the riches of other cultures throughout the world. To become a member of any of our Future of Kulchur tiers is to express your support of such cultural work, and to aid us in continuing it. A unified assemblage of individuals can make a modern Mæcenas and deepen access to radical works.

The Oyster ($2/month)

- Three issues (PDFs) of your choice of our art journal, *Hyperion*.
- 15% discount on all purchases (for orders made directly through our site) during the subscription term (one year).
- Impact: $2 a month contributes to the cost to convert a title to an ebook and make it accessible to wider audiences.

Paris Spleen ($5/month)

- Receive $35 worth of books or your choice from our back catalog.
- Three issues (PDFs) of your choice of our art journal, *Hyperion*.
- 18% discount on all purchases (for orders made directly through our site) during the subscription term (one year).
- Impact: $5 a month contributes to the cost purchasing new fonts for expanding the range of our typesetting palette.

Gilgamesh ($10/month)

- Receive $70 worth books of your choice from our back catalog.
- 4 PDF issues of our magazine *Hyperion*.
- A quarterly newsletter with exclusive content such as interviews with authors or translators, excerpts from upcoming titles, publication news, and more.
- 20% discount on all merchandise (for orders made directly through our site) during the subscription term (one year).
- Select images of our books as they are being typeset.
- Impact: $10 a month contributes to the production and publication of *Hyperion*, encouraging critical engagement with art theory & æsthetics and ensuring we can pay our contributors.

The Greek Music Drama ($25/month)

- Receive $215 worth of books.
- 5 PDF issues of *Hyperion* ($25 value).
- A quarterly newsletter with exclusive content such as interviews with authors or translators, excerpts from upcoming titles, publication news, and more.
- 25% discount (for orders made directly through our site) on all merchandise during the subscription term (one year).
- Impact: $25 a month contributes to the cost of designing and formatting a book.

Citizen Above Suspicion ($50/month)

- Receive $525 worth of books.
- 6 PDF issues of *Hyperion* ($30 value).
- 1 tote.
- A quarterly newsletter with exclusive content such as interviews with authors or translators, excerpts from upcoming titles, publication news, and more.
- 30% discount on all merchandise (for orders made directly through our site) during the subscription term (one year).
- Select one forthcoming book from our catalog and receive it in advance of release to the general public.
- Impact: $50 a month contributes to editorial & proofreading fees.

Casanova ($100/month)

- Receive $1040 worth of books.
- 7 PDF issues of *Hyperion* ($30 value).
- 1 tote.
- A quarterly newsletter with exclusive content such as interviews with authors or translators, excerpts from upcoming titles, publication news, and more.
- 35% discount on all merchandise (for orders made directly through our site) during the subscription term (one year).
- A signed typeset spread from two forthcoming books.
- Select two forthcoming books from our catalog and receive them in advance of release to the general public.
- Impact: $100 a month contributes to the cost of translating a book, therefore supporting a translator in their craft & bringing a new work & perspective to Anglophone audiences.

Cybernetogamic Vampire ($200/month)

- Receive $2020 worth of books.
- 10 PDF issues of *Hyperion* ($50 value).
- 1 tote.
- A quarterly newsletter with exclusive content such as interviews with authors or translators, excerpts from upcoming titles, publication news, and more.
- 40% discount on all merchandise (for orders made directly through our site) during the subscription term (one year).
- A signed typeset spread from four of our forthcoming books.
- The listing of your name in the colophon to a forthcoming book of your choice.
- Select four forthcoming books from our catalog and receive them in advance of release to the general public.
- Impact: $200 a month contributes to general operating expenses of the press, paying for translation rights, and attending book fairs to represent our writers and translators and reach more readers around the world.

To join the Future of Kulchur, visit here:

contramundumpress.com/support-us